"A collection of conversations with myself and the universe"

Piyush Tikku

ISBN

Hardcase 979-8-89363-957-5
Paperback 979-8-89322-650-8

Dedicated To

Cosmos, ma future femme & myself.

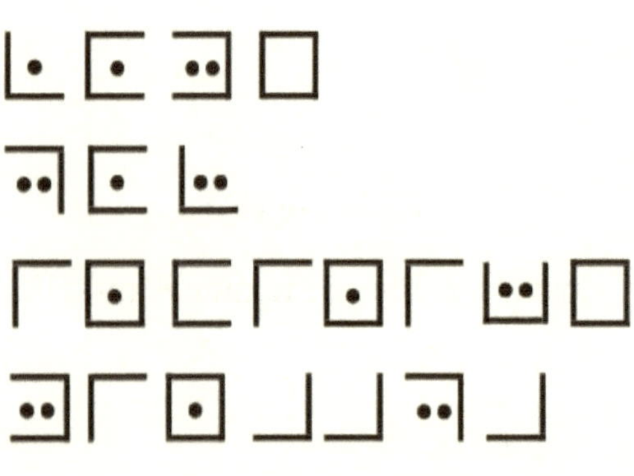

Acknowledgement

I want to thank my maternal uncle Mr Rajesh Raina for his constant unconditional support, love & guidance.

Special thanks to Mr Connor Devine for proofreading & foreword.

Thanks to my mom, dad, sister, Vin, Amir, Shoaib & Sushant for always being there for me & supporting me.

Thanks to all the people who I came across in my life & for the experiences that came with them.

Thanks to Waseem and Notion press team for helping out with marketing & publishing of this book.

Above all I want to thank Radha-Krishna, Shiv-Shakti, my ancestors & the entire cosmos for guiding me & blessing me.

Foreword

It is often said that poetry, in its truest form, can be a window to the soul – a medium for solace, reflection, and a connection to the human experience. It is within these lines, where emotion and memory meet, that we discover who we truly are.

When I first met Piyush, in Auroville, Tamil Nadu in 2023. I was struck by his sincerity and openness of heart. These traits are discernible within the poems you will read within these pages. Discernible, too is the theme of darkness, which runs throughout the collection. Be it in the "depths of darkness" in *Convalescence from Darkness*; the "words echoed from the shadows" in *Undying;* silence "shadowed by tears of despair" in *Shattered Silence*; or the "wings of death" we see in *Death*.

The ideas of hopelessness and despair are ever-present in many of the poems you will read here. *Shattered* speaks of "broken dreams" piercing the soul, and we are made to feel all too keenly the pain of the wretched creature "bound by chains of miseries and despair" in *Deliverance.* We do not have to search hard to find the sadness within these pages.

Yet, while the collection is infused with an undeniable melancholic twinge (indeed, "melancholy" is a word that features prominently), it is counterpoised by another idea: that of hope. If we work hard enough, we can find within these pages a sense of light, redemption and, ultimately, happiness.

Often this is tied to the idea of a "beloved", an unknown or unseen source of love which is recurrent throughout much of the poetry contained within. *Ambrosia Inamorata* exhorts this "beloved" to "quench the thirst of this soul", and *Mon Sanctuary* call on the "beloved" to "be my temple".

Whether our own personal "beloved" is a person, an idea, a feeling, or something else entirely, one gets the sense that the writer has left this to us to determine. But we are left with an undeniable sense that, just like saplings can sprout from the dirt and become trees, so too can love be nurtured in the darkest of places.

As you read these poems, you may find yourself wondering where your own beloved lies. *Seeker* tells us "The truth he seeks is within him" – perhaps that is the ultimate message of this collection. The truth is within all of us.

Connor Devine

Civil Servant

February 2024

Connor Devine is a Civil Servant in the UK, a former teacher and student of English, and a lover of poetry.

Contents

Contents

Winds of Reminiscence

Winter winds touching my hair,
Reminding me of yesteryears,
Melancholy filling my heart
In disbelief of all that's lost.

Deliverance

Amidst the darkness it searched for light,
bound by chains of miseries & despair
it wanted to fly,
the wings were broken & it released a
painful clamour,
even the skies started to cry for its longing.

Sanguineness

During cold winter nights,
the moon shimmers its light,
giving hope to lonesome souls.

Perseverance

I want to blend into you,
In the existence of your being.
Maybe it's dark,
Maybe it's an asylum of broken dreams.

Convalescence From Darkness

He found her in the depths of darkness,
broken into a million pieces.
He collected all of them one by one
And tried fixing them with his light.
It was arduous,
It was heartrending,
Yet, he didn't relinquish.
For he wanted to fix her
And make her whole again.

Undying

Her words echoed from the shadows,
piercing right through his heart.
It kept on piercing until there was nothing left,
apart from an undying hollowness within his soul.

Wandering Homme Fou

Was thee lost to be found again

or

was thee lost to get lost again.

In the middle of nothingness,

all thou found was bloodshed & chaos.

A horrifying madness that thou couldn't fathom.

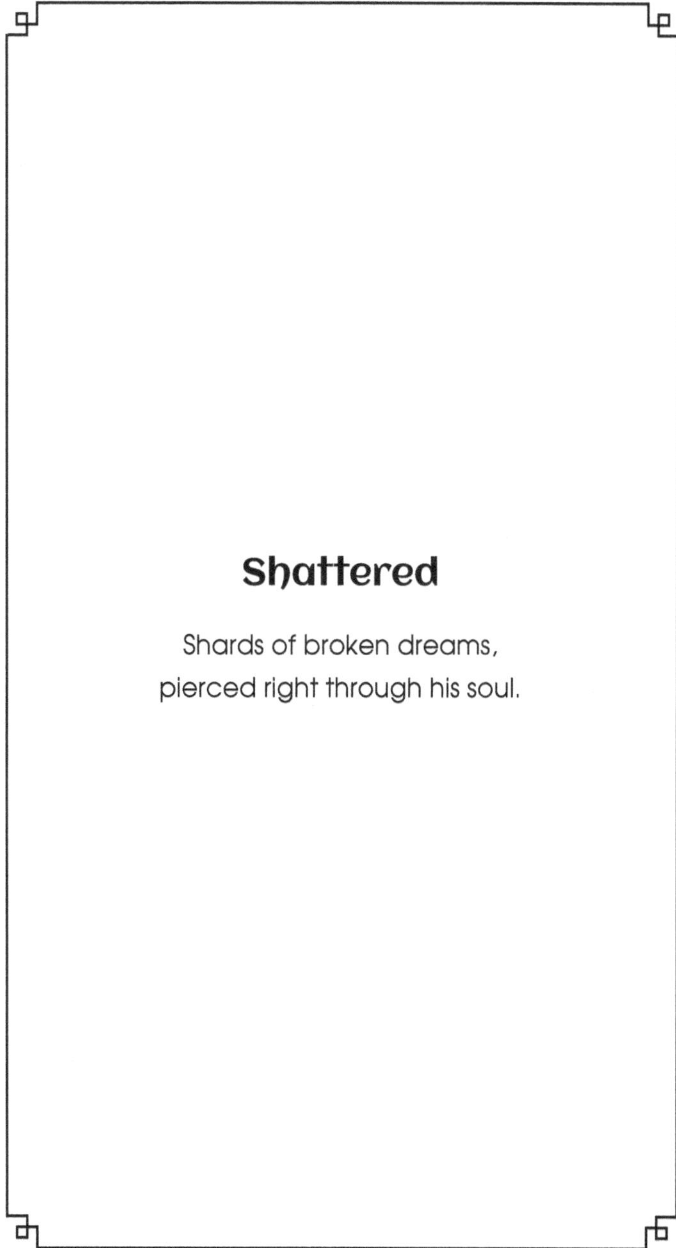

Shattered

Shards of broken dreams,
pierced right through his soul.

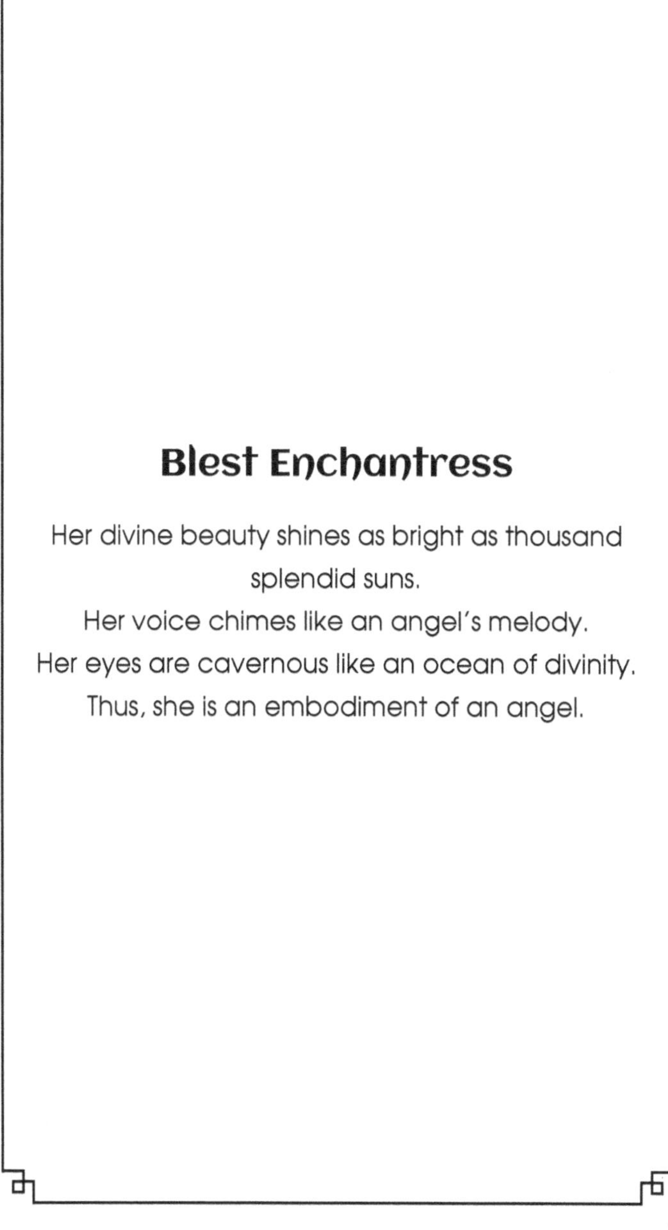

Blest Enchantress

Her divine beauty shines as bright as thousand
splendid suns.
Her voice chimes like an angel's melody.
Her eyes are cavernous like an ocean of divinity.
Thus, she is an embodiment of an angel.

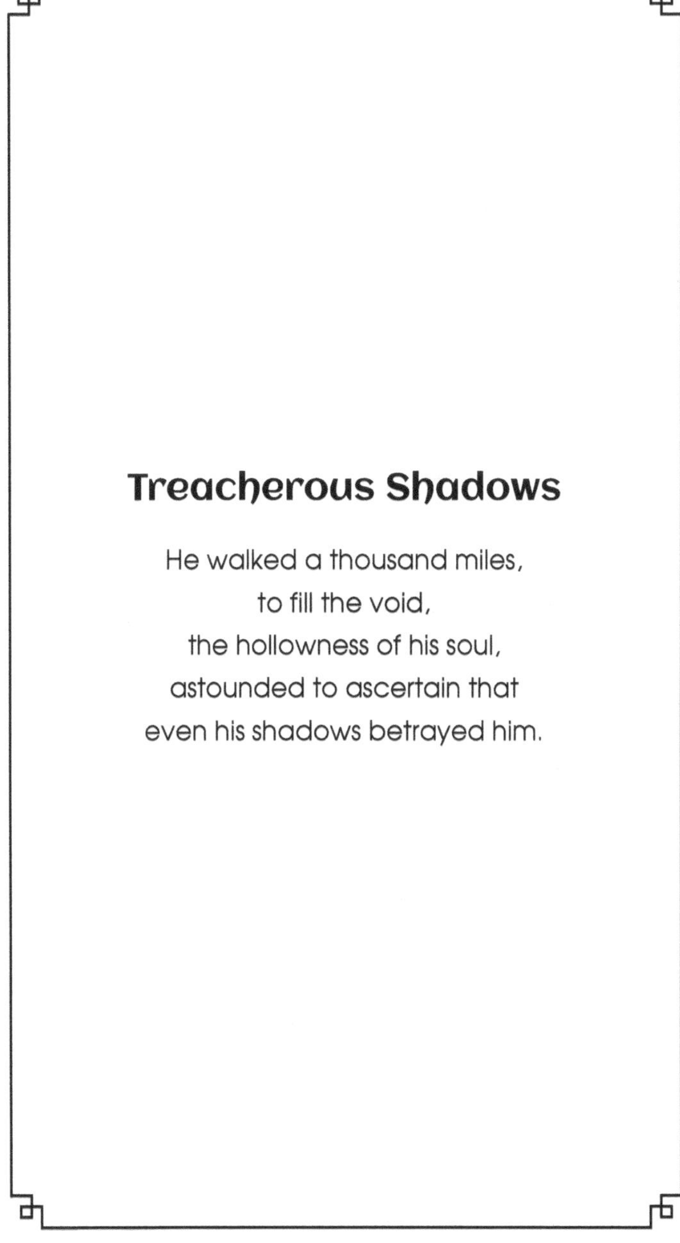

Treacherous Shadows

He walked a thousand miles,
to fill the void,
the hollowness of his soul,
astounded to ascertain that
even his shadows betrayed him.

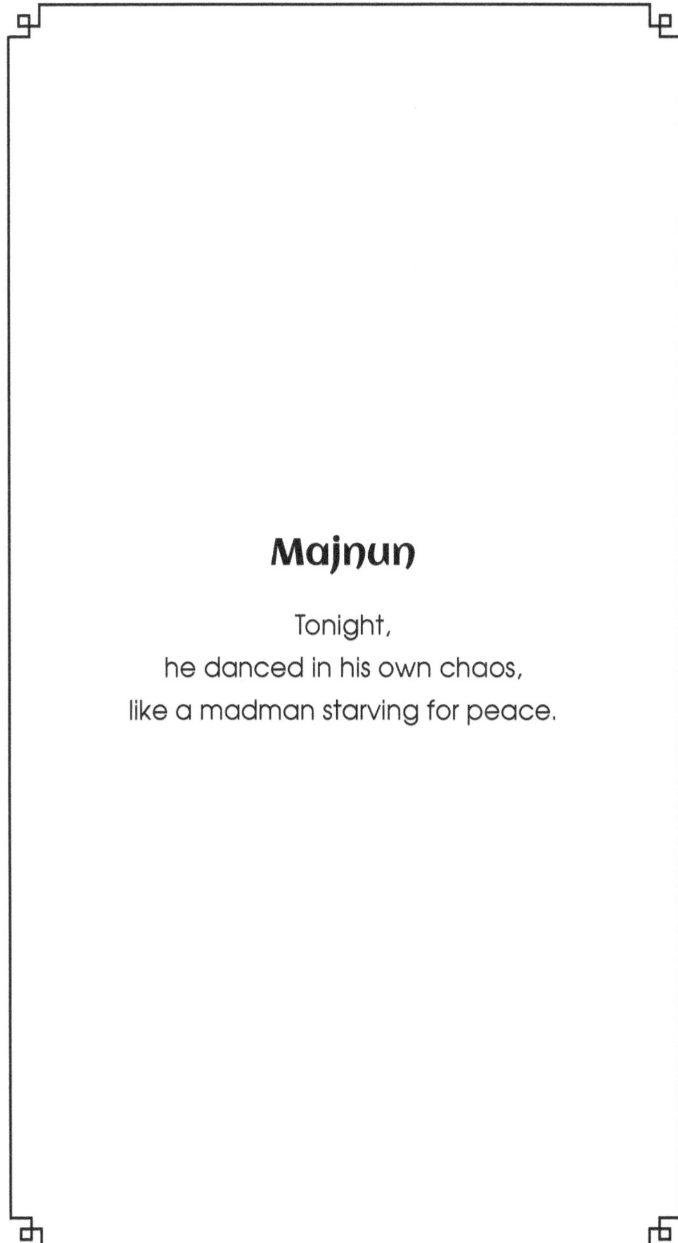

Majnun

Tonight,
he danced in his own chaos,
like a madman starving for peace.

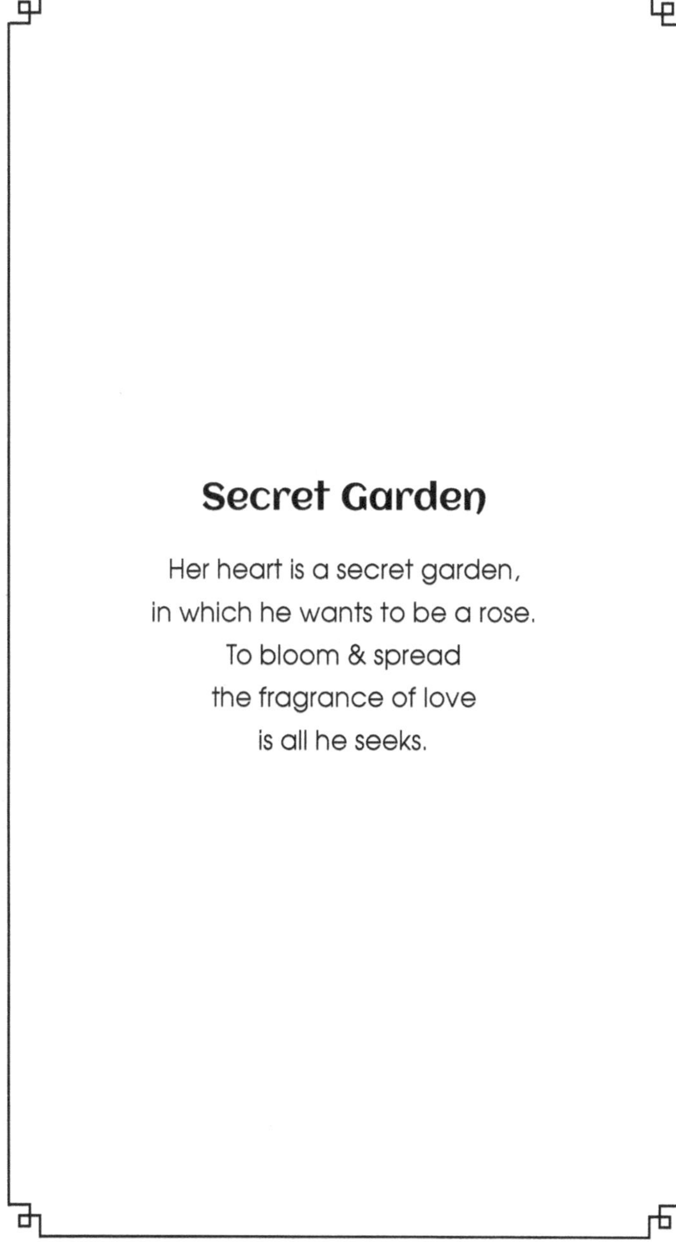

Secret Garden

Her heart is a secret garden,
in which he wants to be a rose.
To bloom & spread
the fragrance of love
is all he seeks.

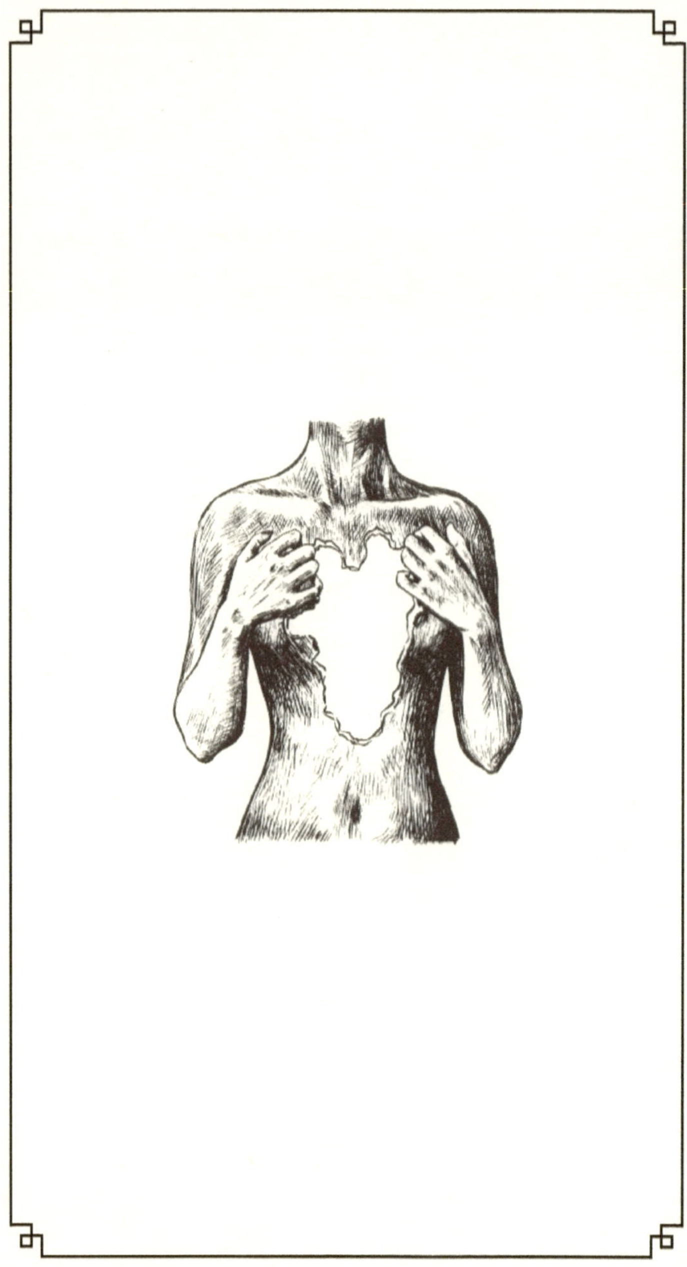

Puppet of Mud

His soul clenched in ruthless claws of despair,
his heart by demons of the past.
All that's left of him is
A hollowed puppet of mud.

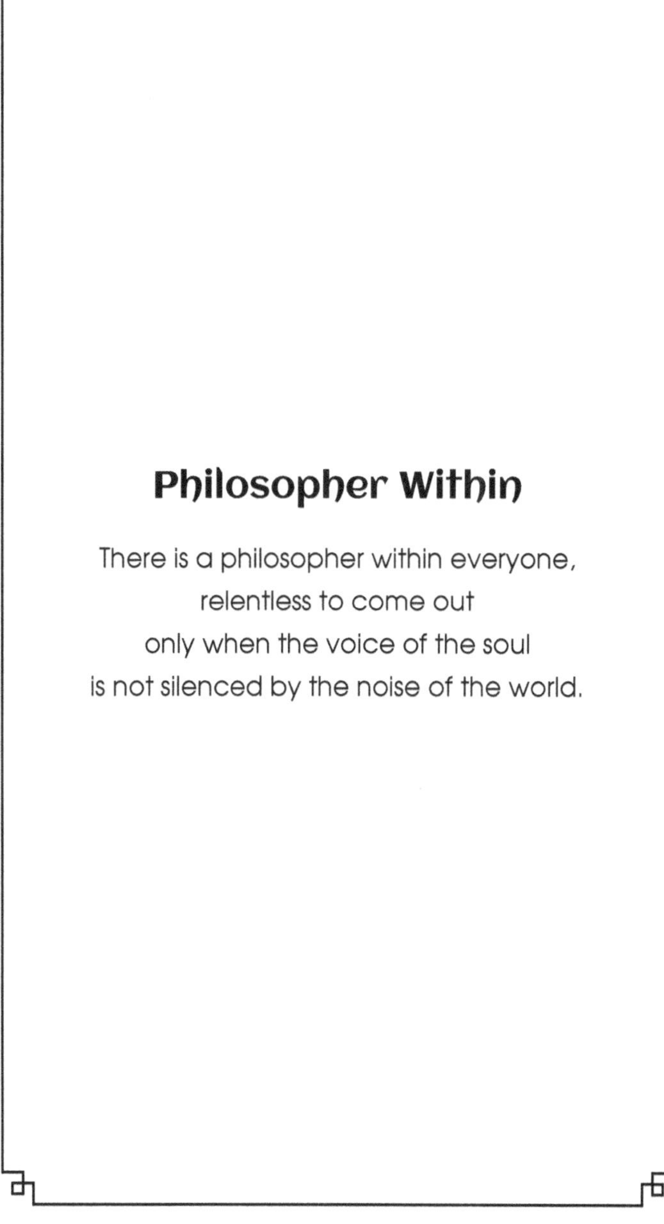

Philosopher Within

There is a philosopher within everyone,
relentless to come out
only when the voice of the soul
is not silenced by the noise of the world.

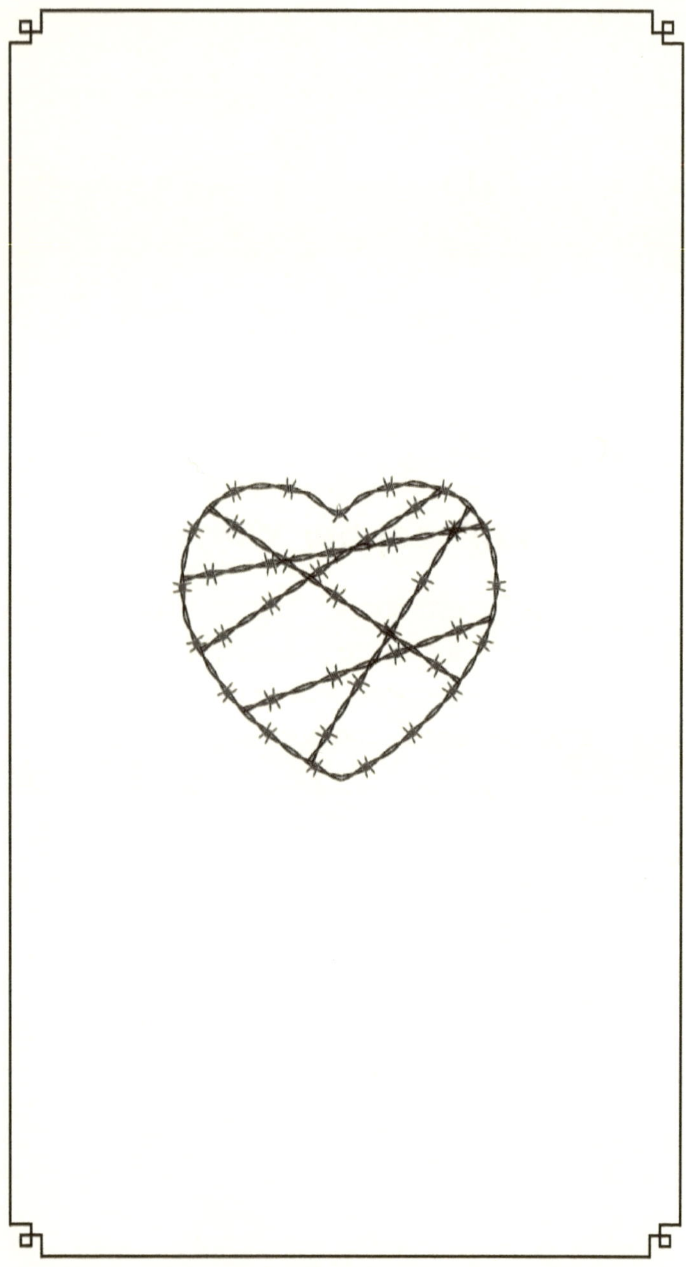

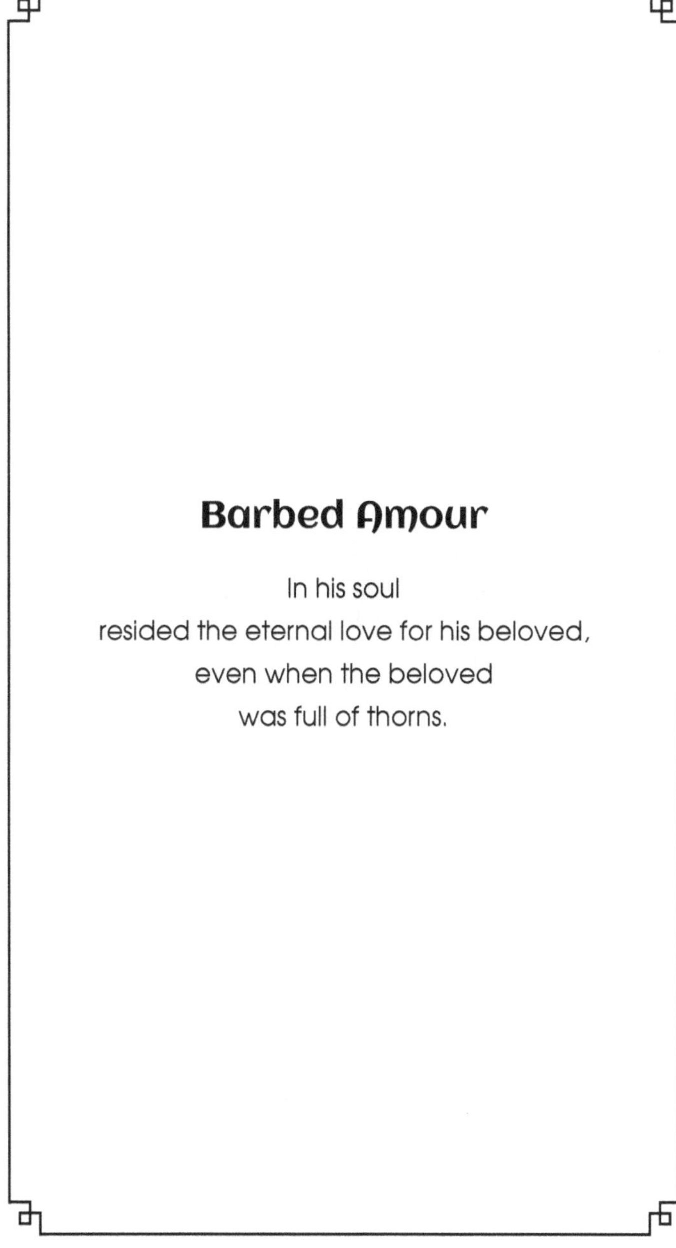

Barbed Amour

In his soul
resided the eternal love for his beloved,
even when the beloved
was full of thorns.

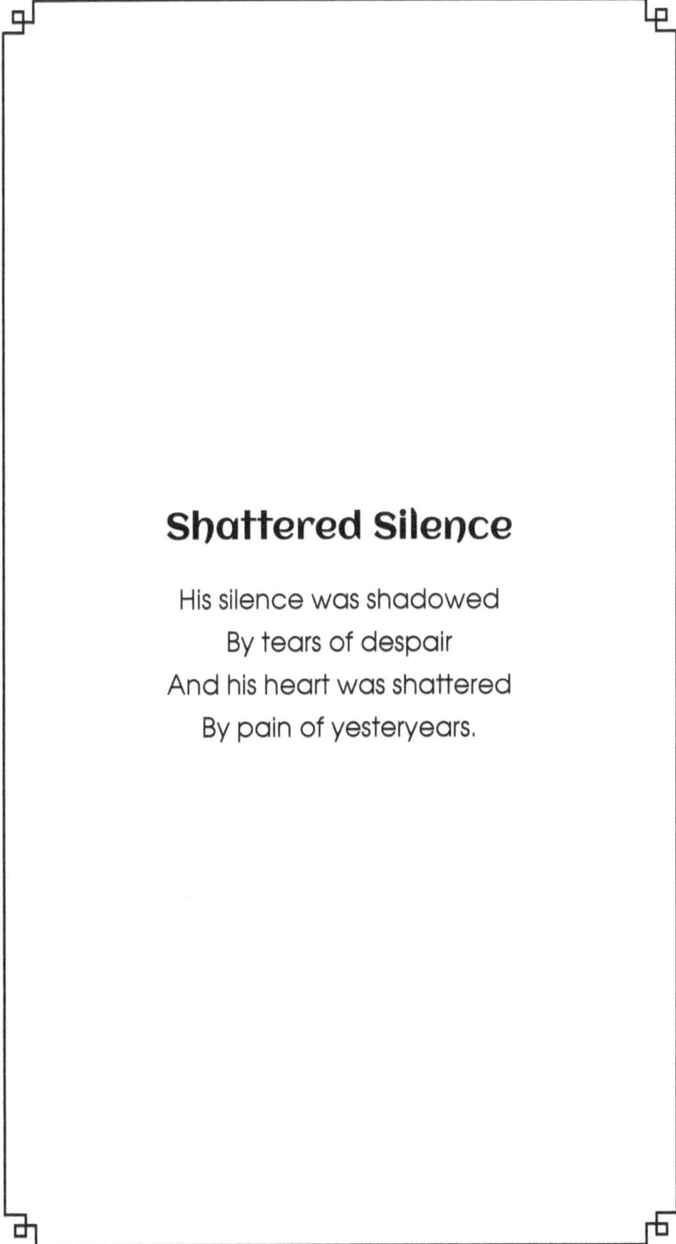

Shattered Silence

His silence was shadowed
By tears of despair
And his heart was shattered
By pain of yesteryears.

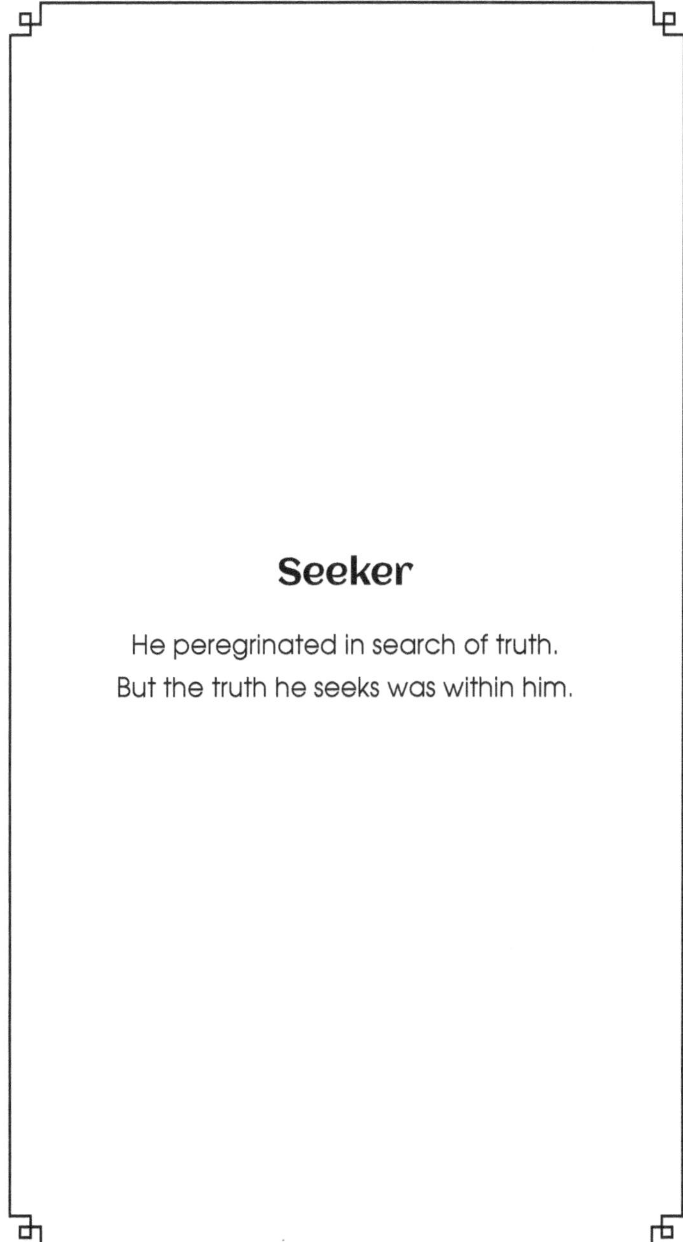

Seeker

He peregrinated in search of truth.
But the truth he seeks was within him.

Strings of Melancholy

The strings of melancholy engulfed his heart,
reminding him of yesteryears.
Tears, pain & broken heart is all he recalled.

Lone Wolf

His heart yearned for beloved,
Like a wolf yearning for moon.

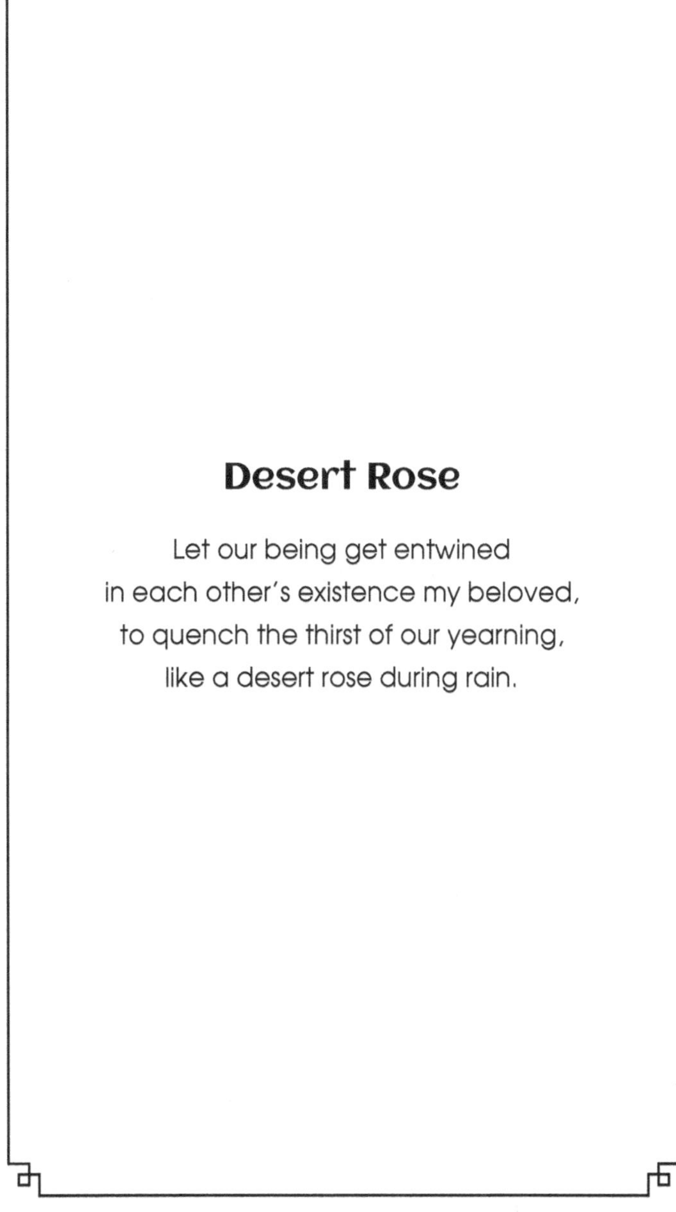

Desert Rose

Let our being get entwined
in each other's existence my beloved,
to quench the thirst of our yearning,
like a desert rose during rain.

Death

Like a wind it came & whispered in his ears,
I have come to take you away
from the sufferings of yesteryears.
His eyes glistened
as he clenched to the wings of death,
like a child clenching to his mother.

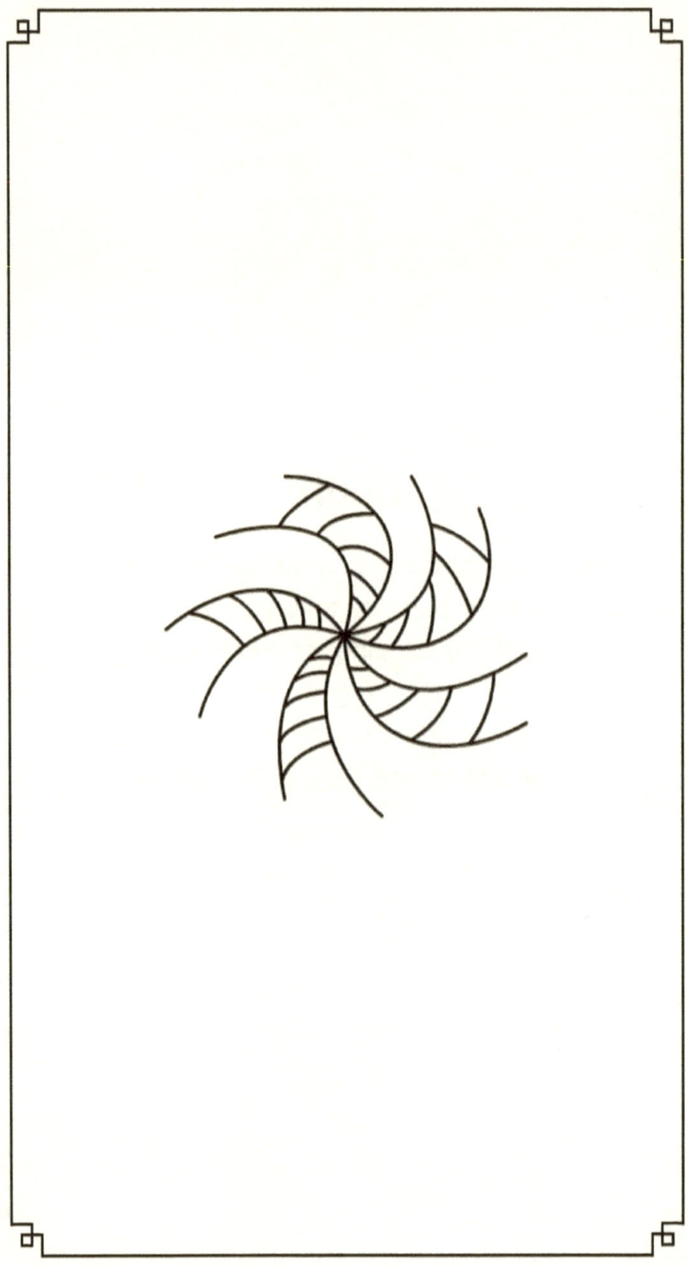

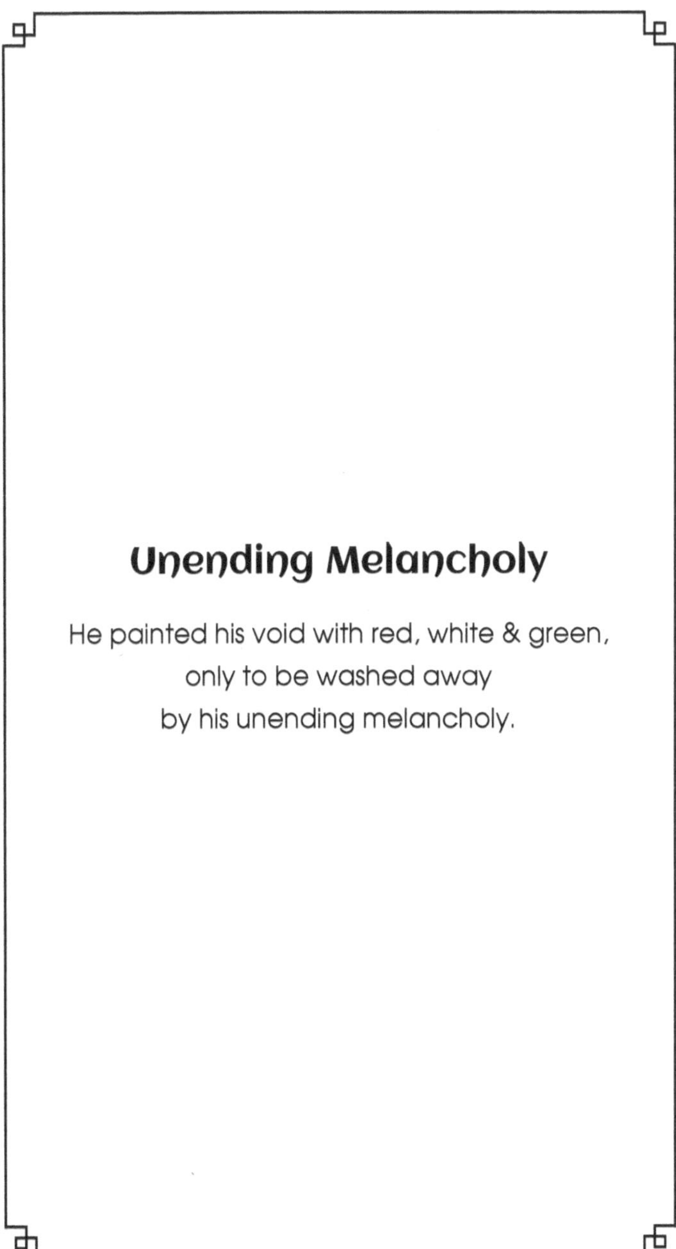

Unending Melancholy

He painted his void with red, white & green,
only to be washed away
by his unending melancholy.

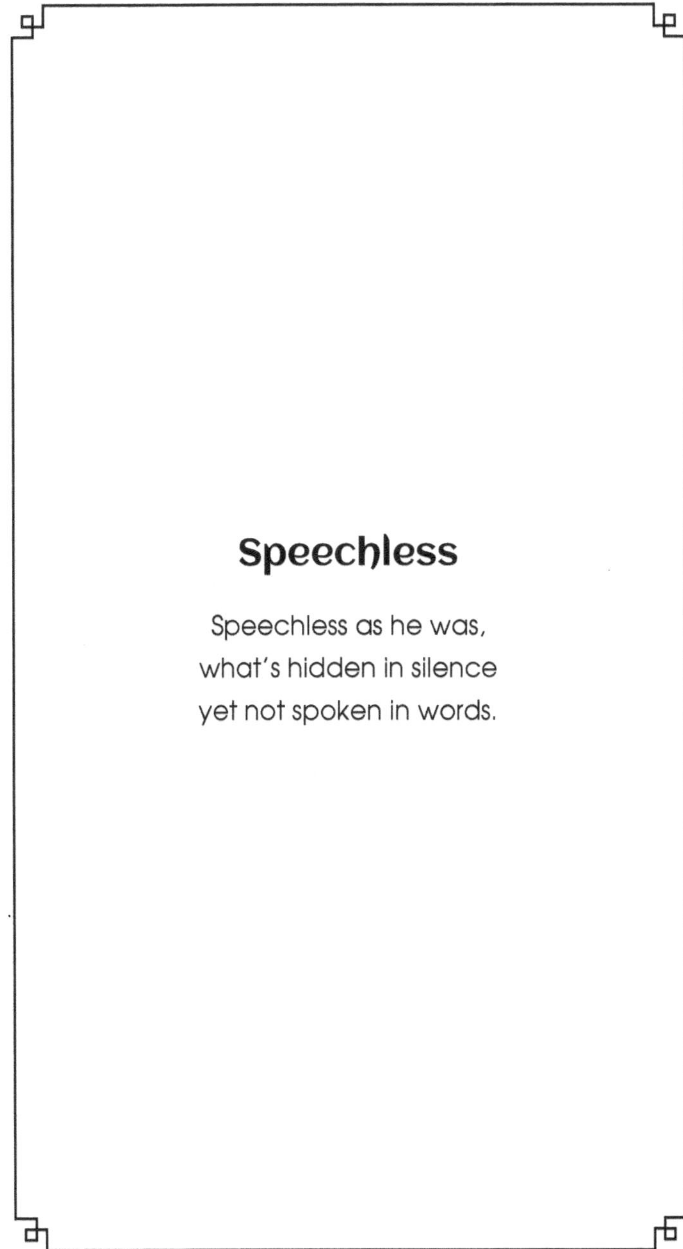

Speechless

Speechless as he was,
what's hidden in silence
yet not spoken in words.

Tragicomedy

He screamed,
he cried,
he begged.
The curtains fell,
the play ended
but his pain didn't.

Symphony of Lost

His soul feels the symphony of emotions,
engulfing him.
Not knowing what to feel.
Despair?
Harmony?
Heartbreak?
Pain?
Happiness?
Joy?
Lost, is what he is.

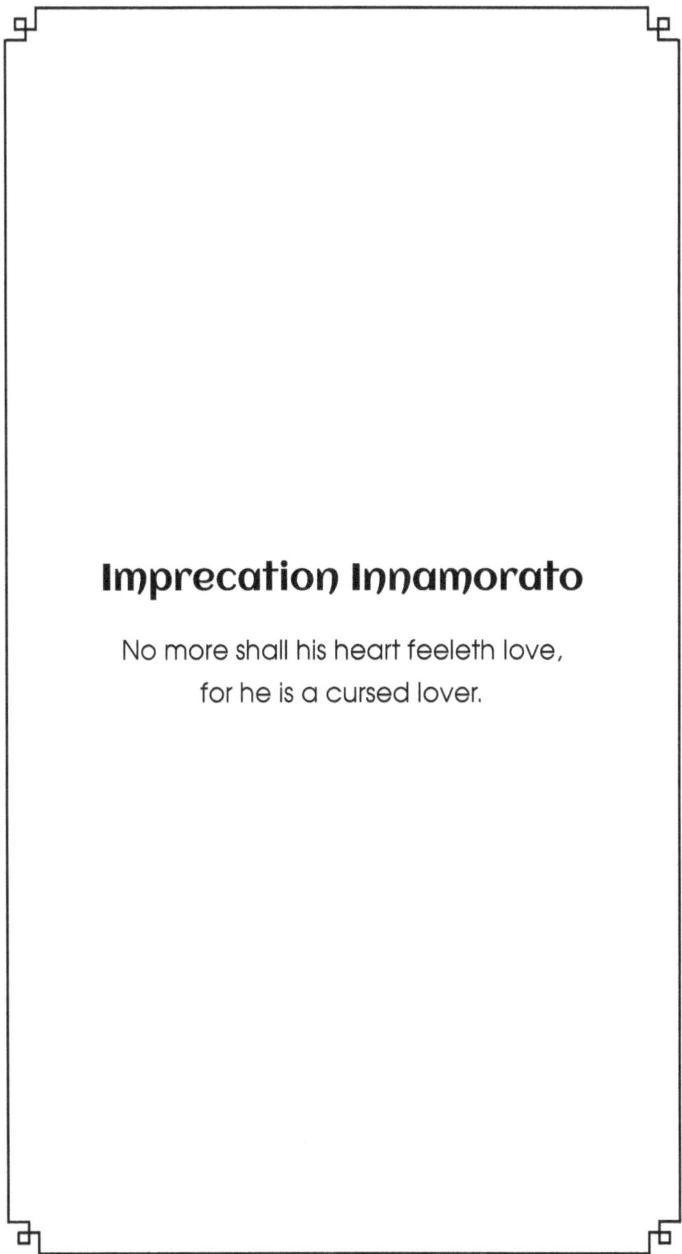

Imprecation Innamorato

No more shall his heart feeleth love,
for he is a cursed lover.

Elixir

Her love is an elixir to his soul,
but yet he can't.
For he is a cursed lover.

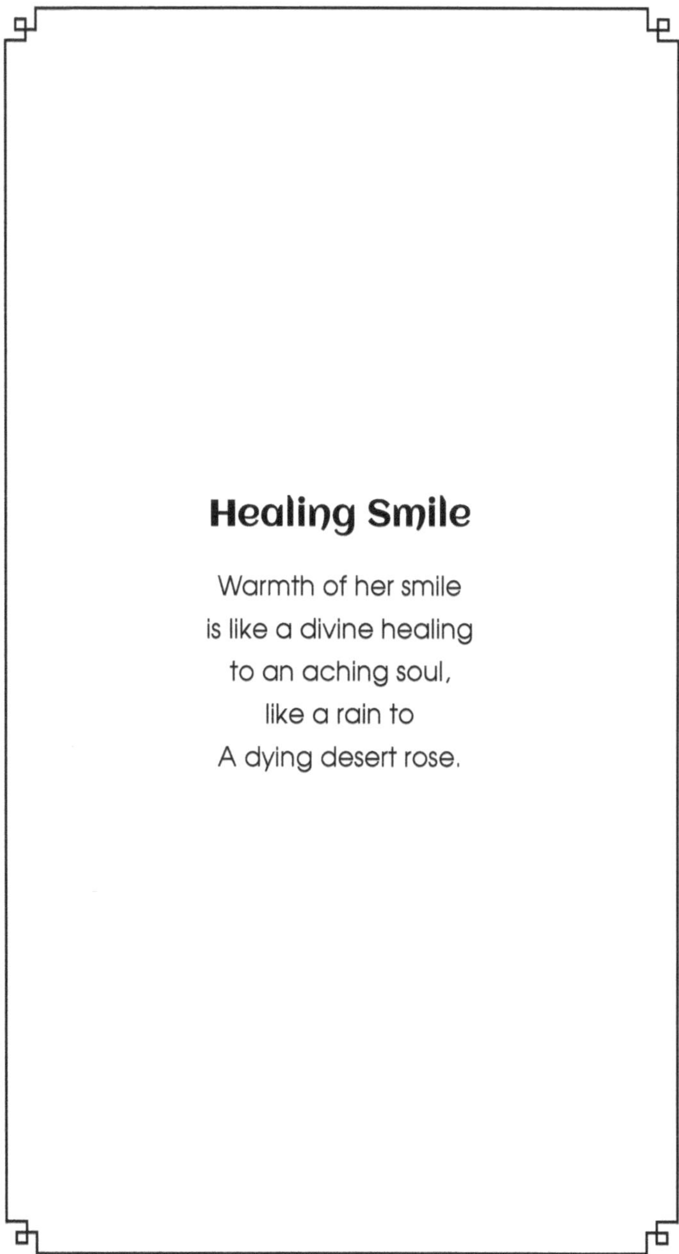

Healing Smile

Warmth of her smile
is like a divine healing
to an aching soul,
like a rain to
A dying desert rose.

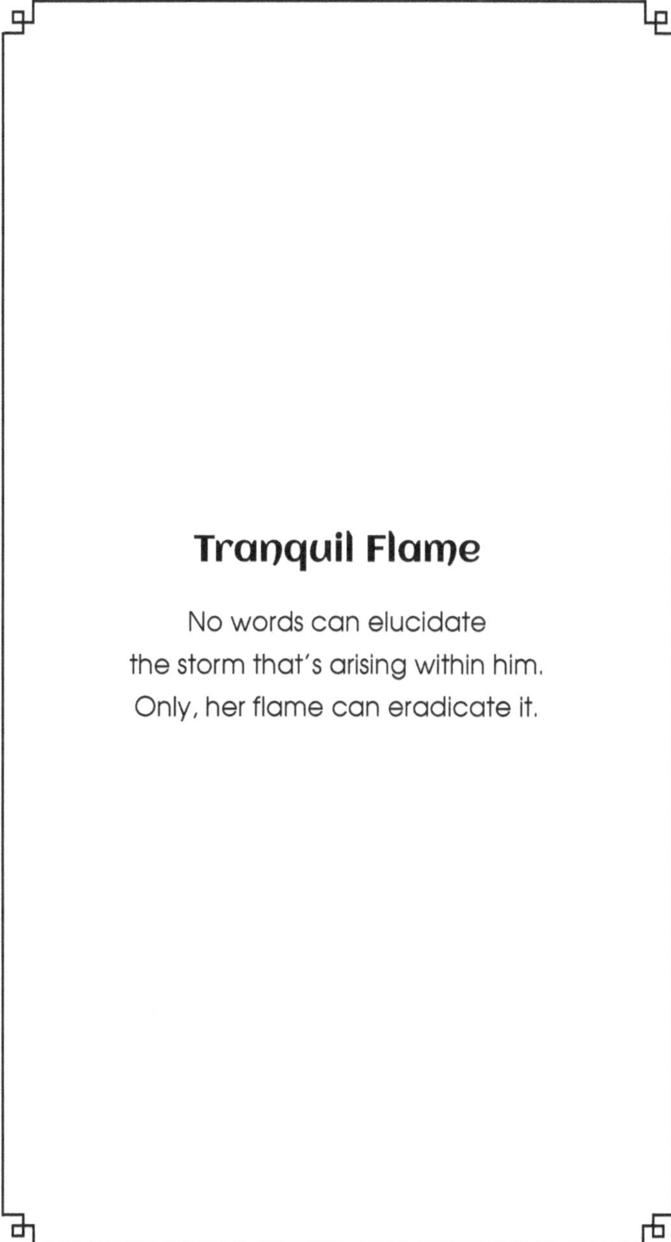

Tranquil Flame

No words can elucidate
the storm that's arising within him.
Only, her flame can eradicate it.

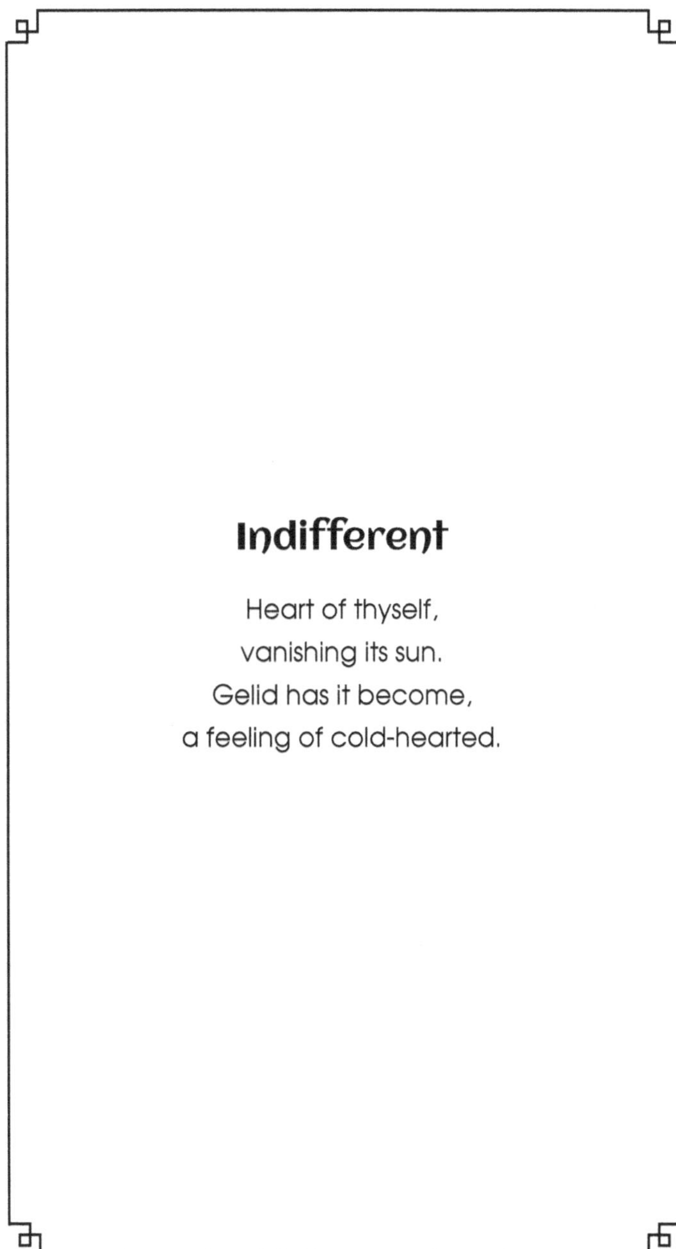

Indifferent

Heart of thyself,
vanishing its sun.
Gelid has it become,
a feeling of cold-hearted.

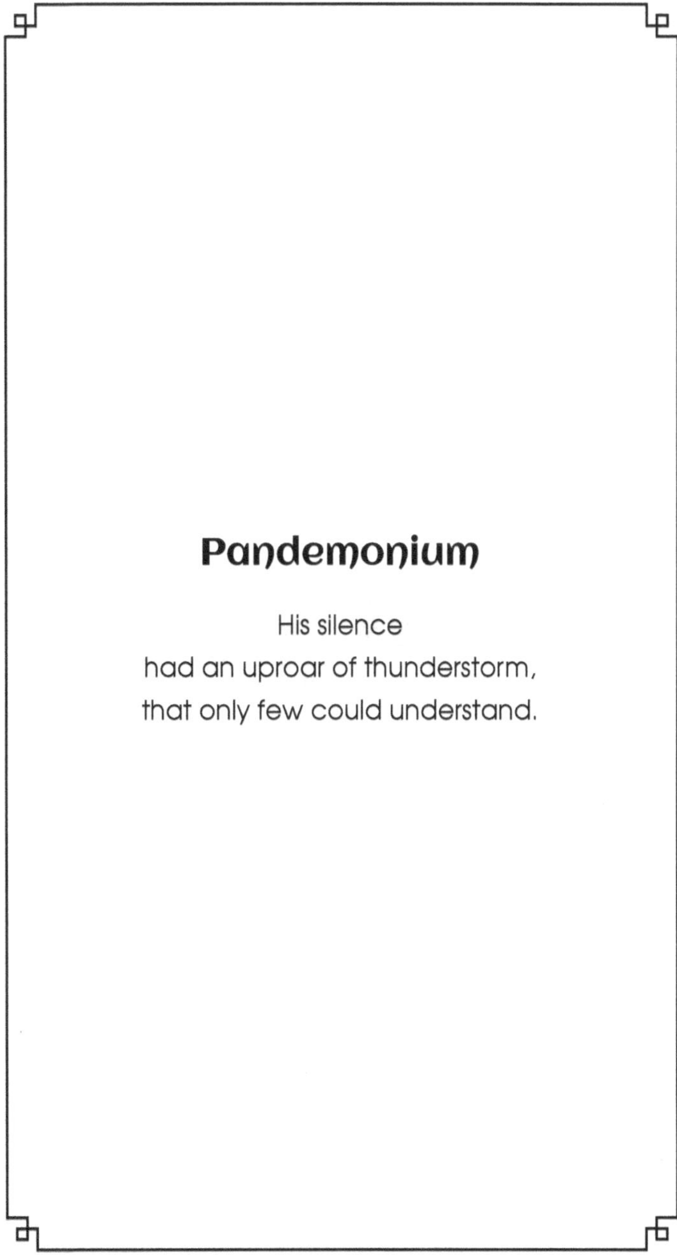

Pandemonium

His silence
had an uproar of thunderstorm,
that only few could understand.

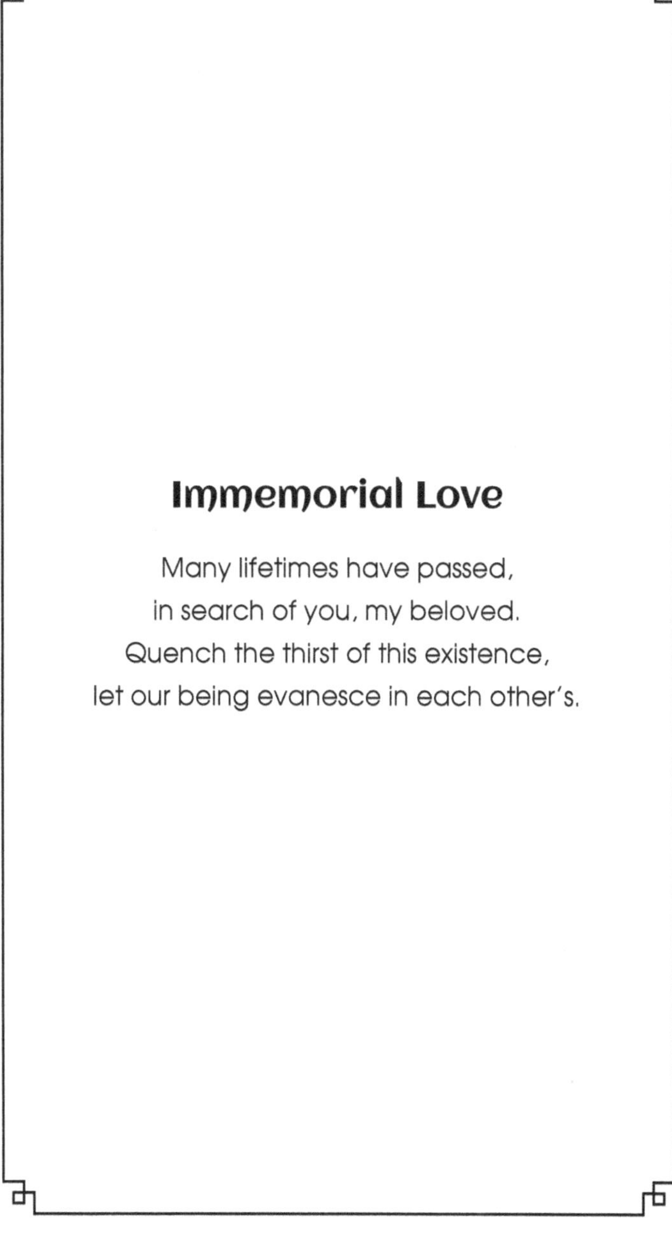

Immemorial Love

Many lifetimes have passed,
in search of you, my beloved.
Quench the thirst of this existence,
let our being evanesce in each other's.

Divine Convergence

Like a moon,

you are far away from me.

Untouched,

yet my heart feels profound amour.

Let my being immerse,

under your glistening moonlight.

To feel,

the divinity of your being.

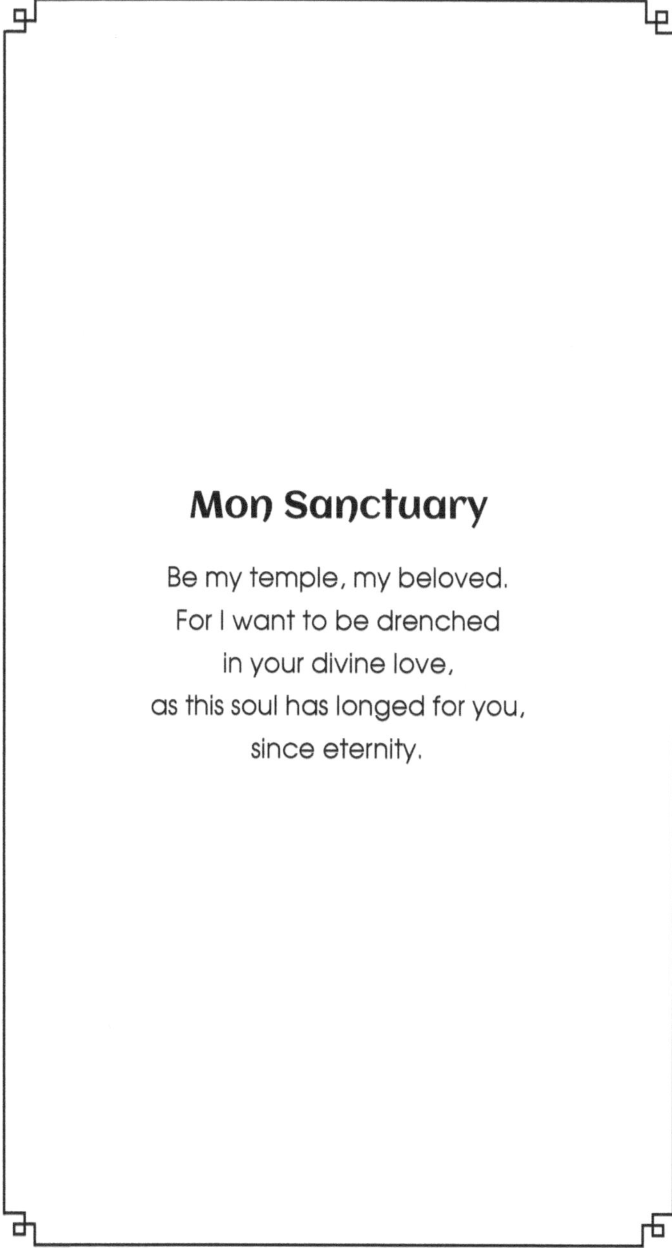

Mon Sanctuary

Be my temple, my beloved.
For I want to be drenched
in your divine love,
as this soul has longed for you,
since eternity.

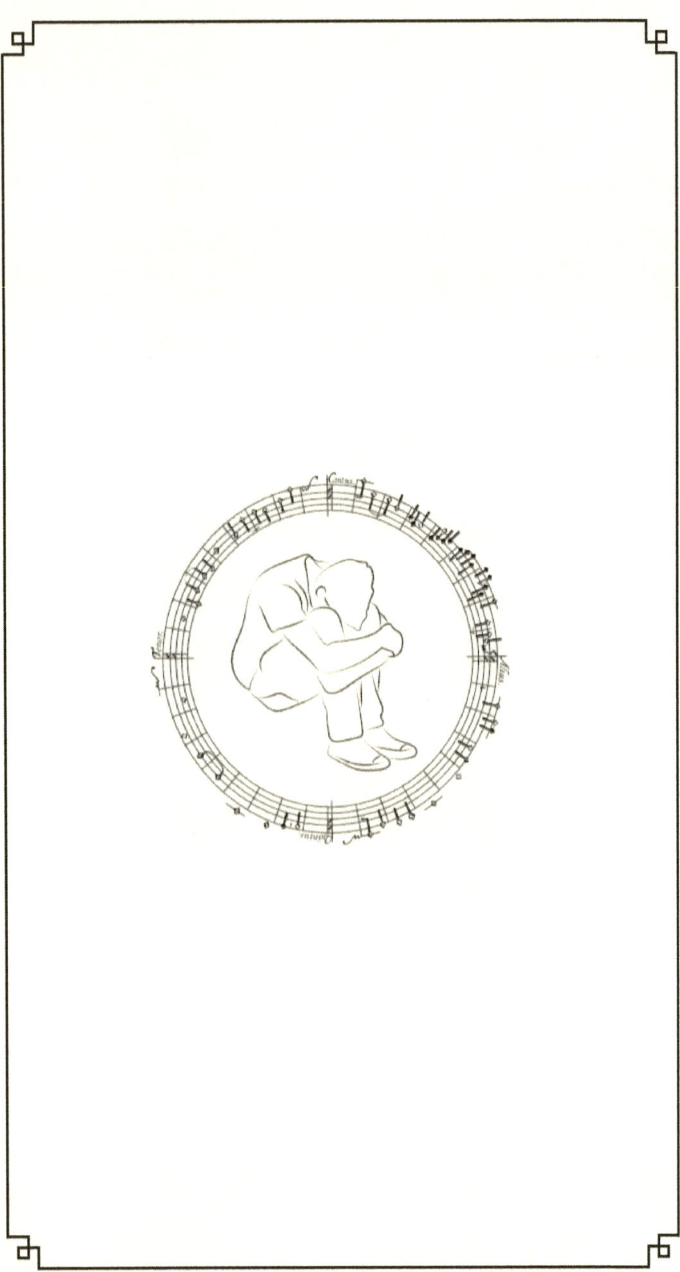

Bittersweet Symphony

His silence
sang the bittersweet symphony
of the scars from yesteryears,
which were trapped
deep within his being.

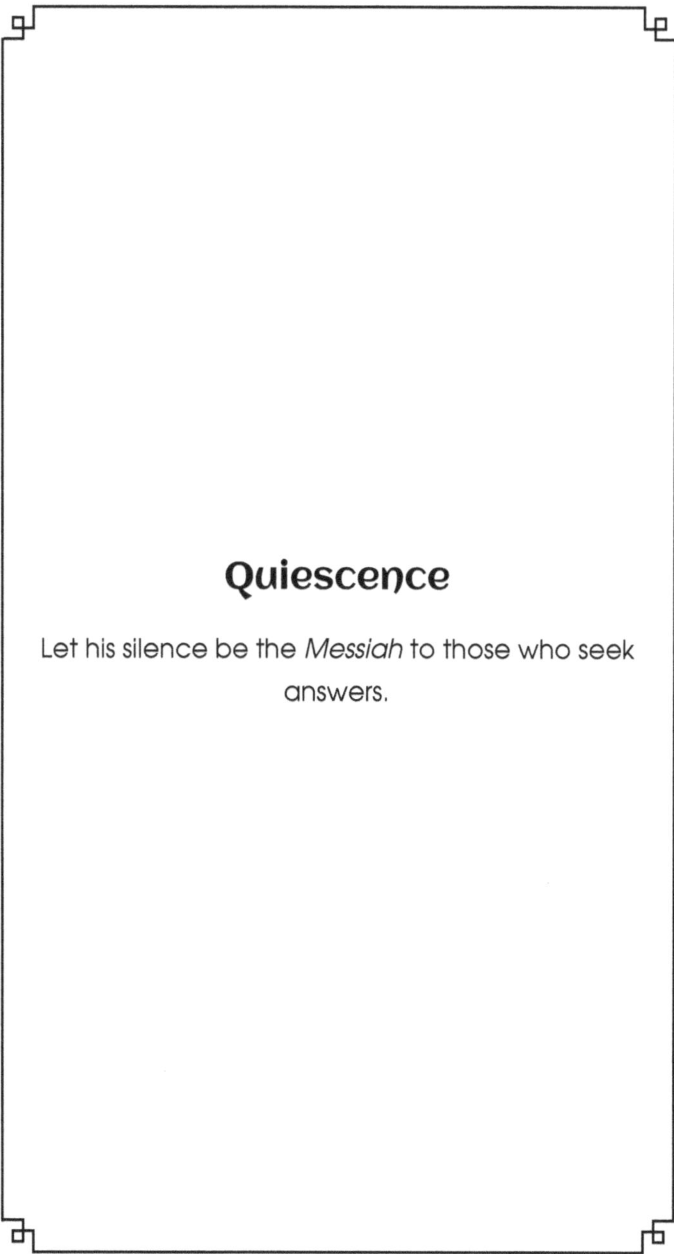

Quiescence

Let his silence be the *Messiah* to those who seek answers.

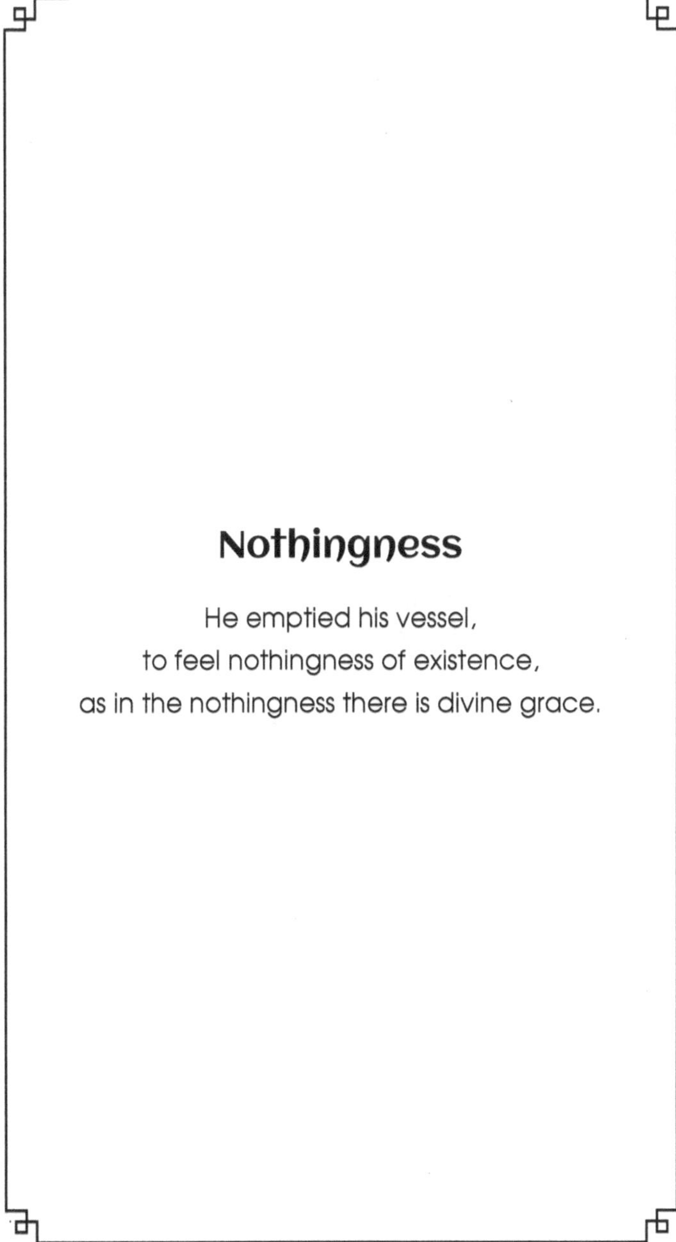

Nothingness

He emptied his vessel,
to feel nothingness of existence,
as in the nothingness there is divine grace.

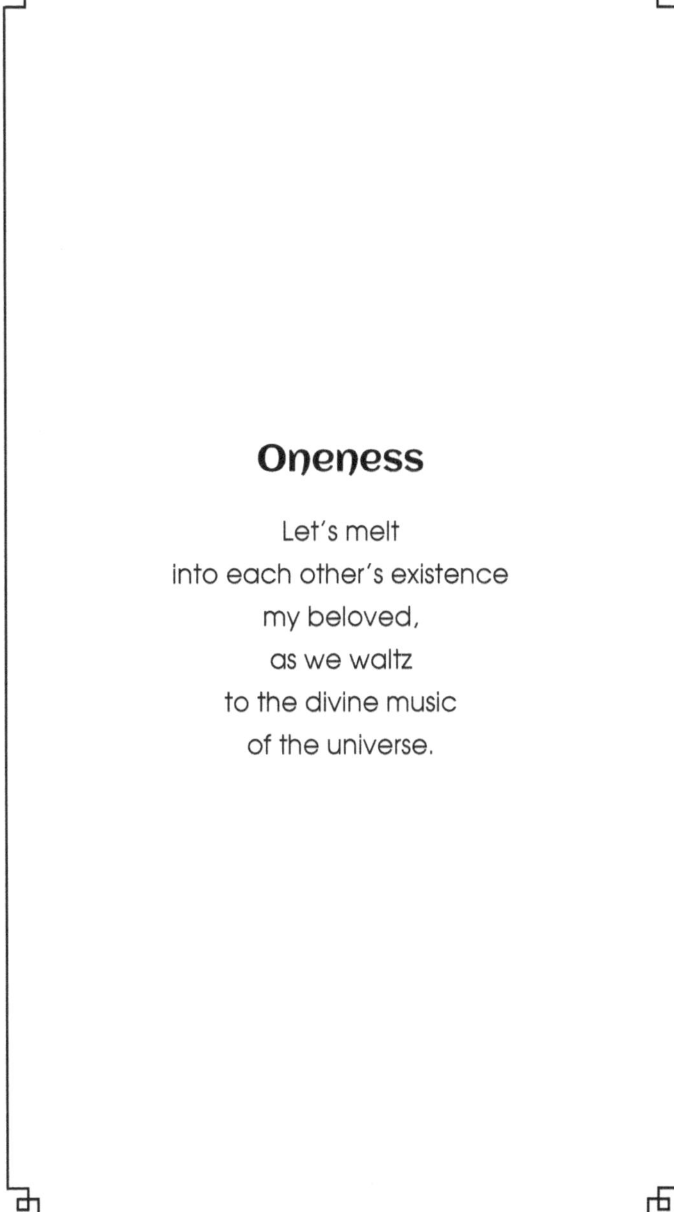

Oneness

Let's melt
into each other's existence
my beloved,
as we waltz
to the divine music
of the universe.

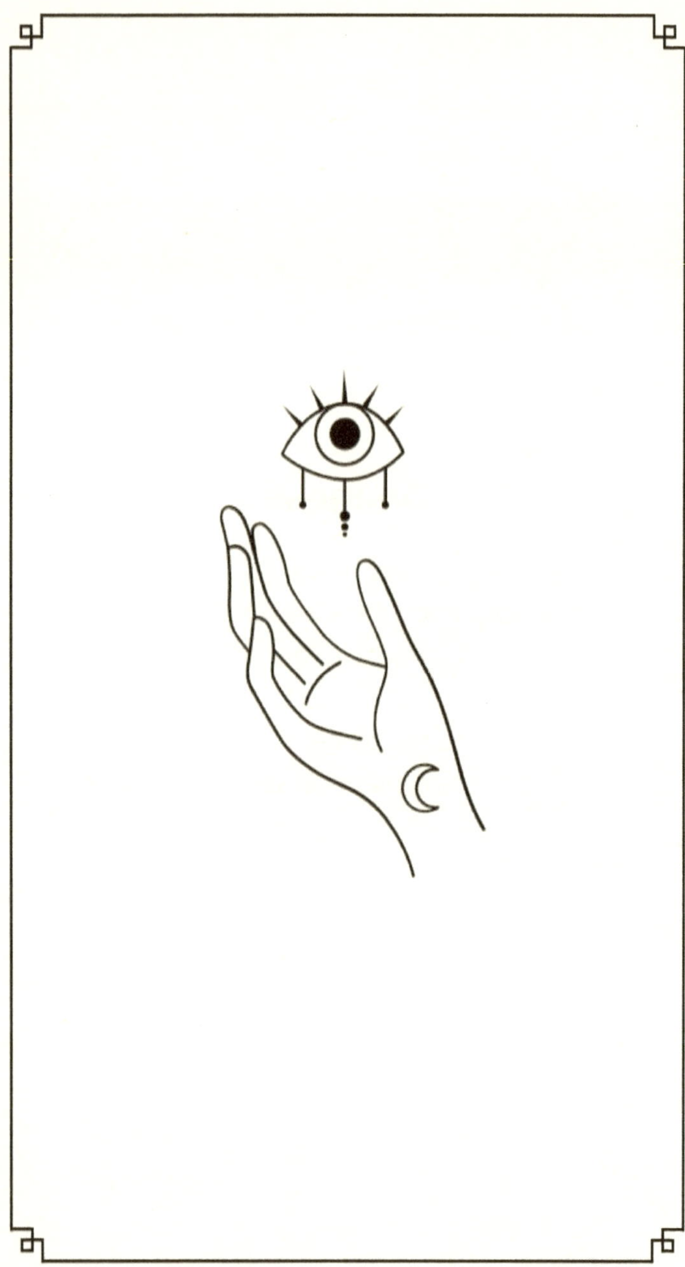

Invigorating

Let the anguish of his soul,
become the sanctum of his awakening.

Countenancing Largesse

Let me endure
this unending anguish my beloved,
for it's a gift of your love.

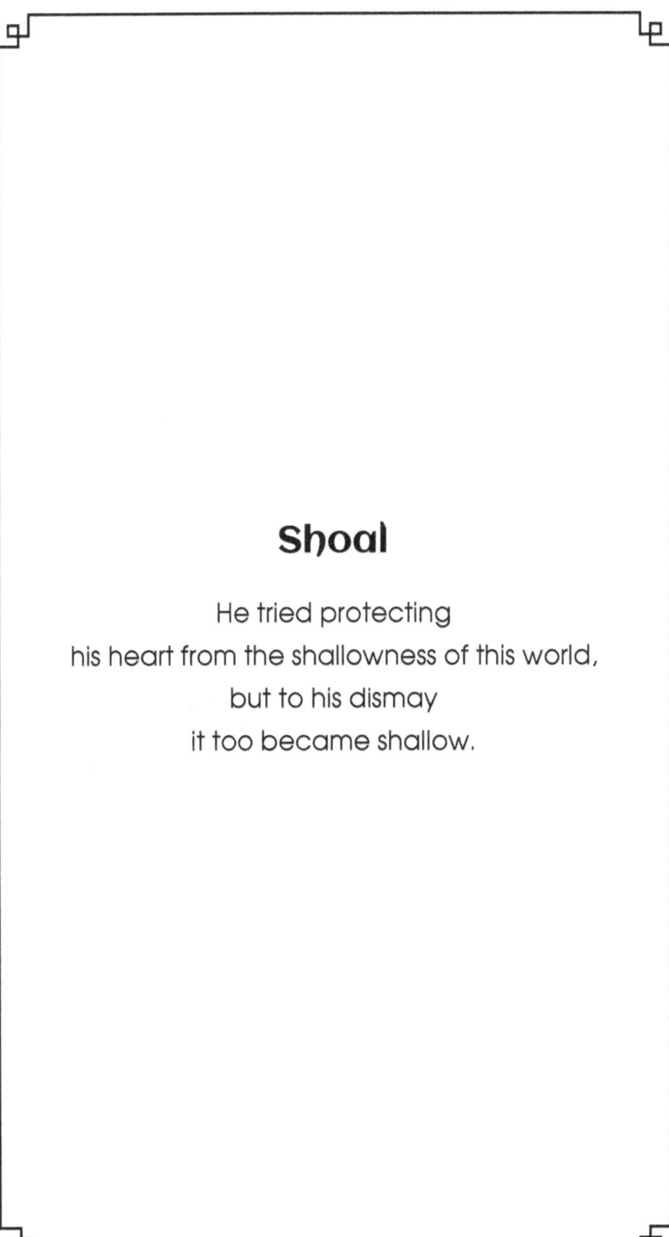

Shoal

He tried protecting
his heart from the shallowness of this world,
but to his dismay
it too became shallow.

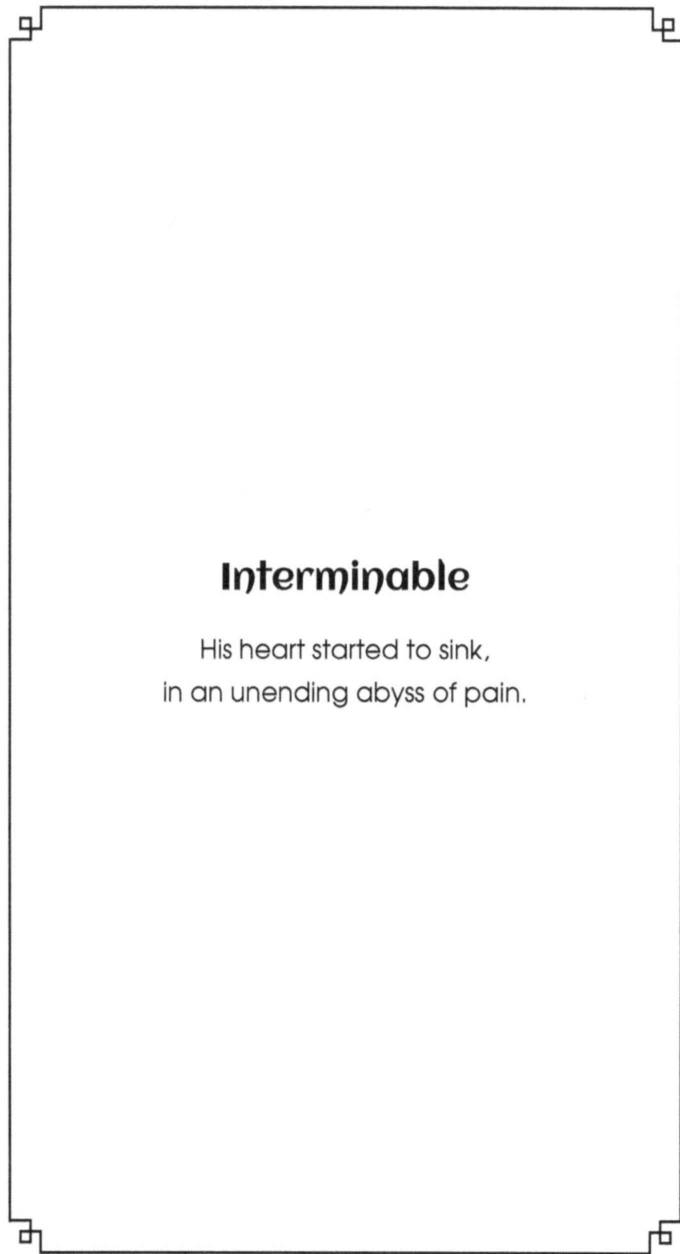

Interminable

His heart started to sink,
in an unending abyss of pain.

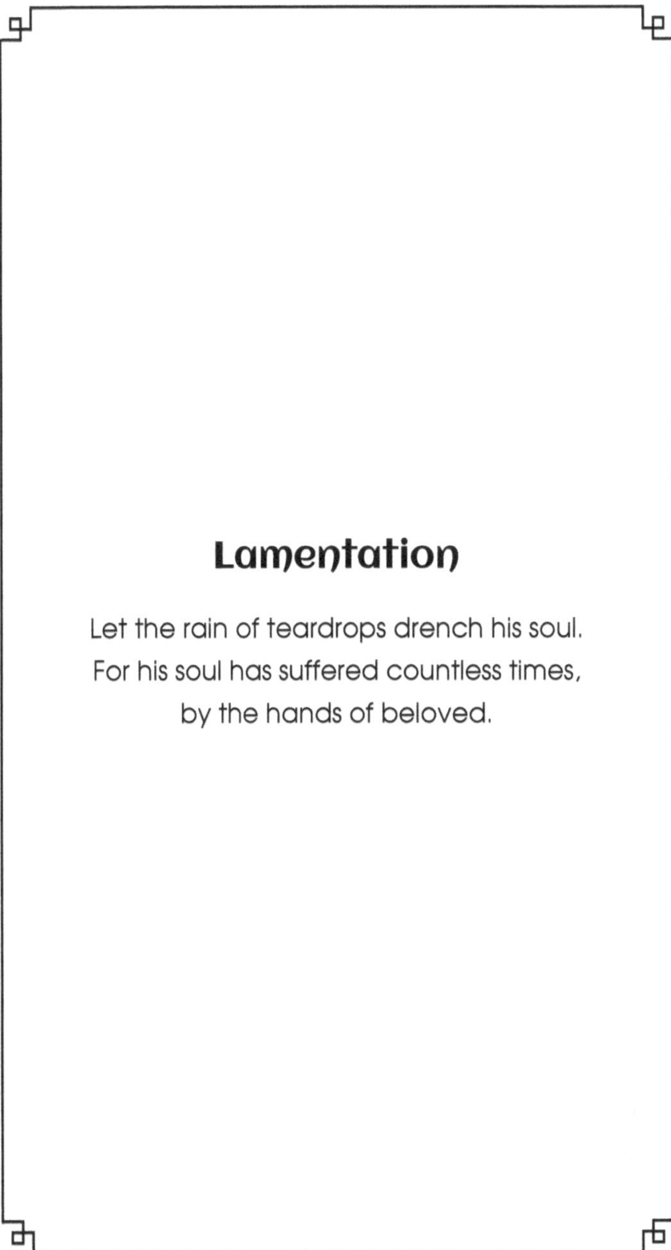

Lamentation

Let the rain of teardrops drench his soul.
For his soul has suffered countless times,
by the hands of beloved.

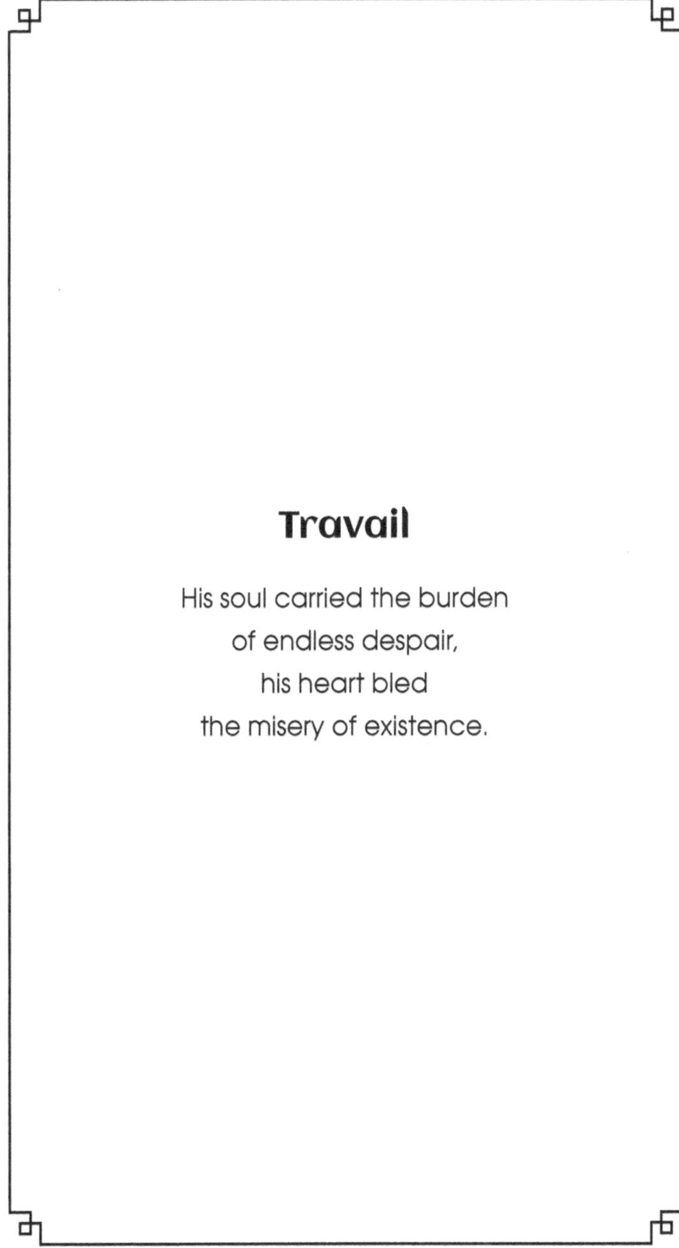

Travail

His soul carried the burden
of endless despair,
his heart bled
the misery of existence.

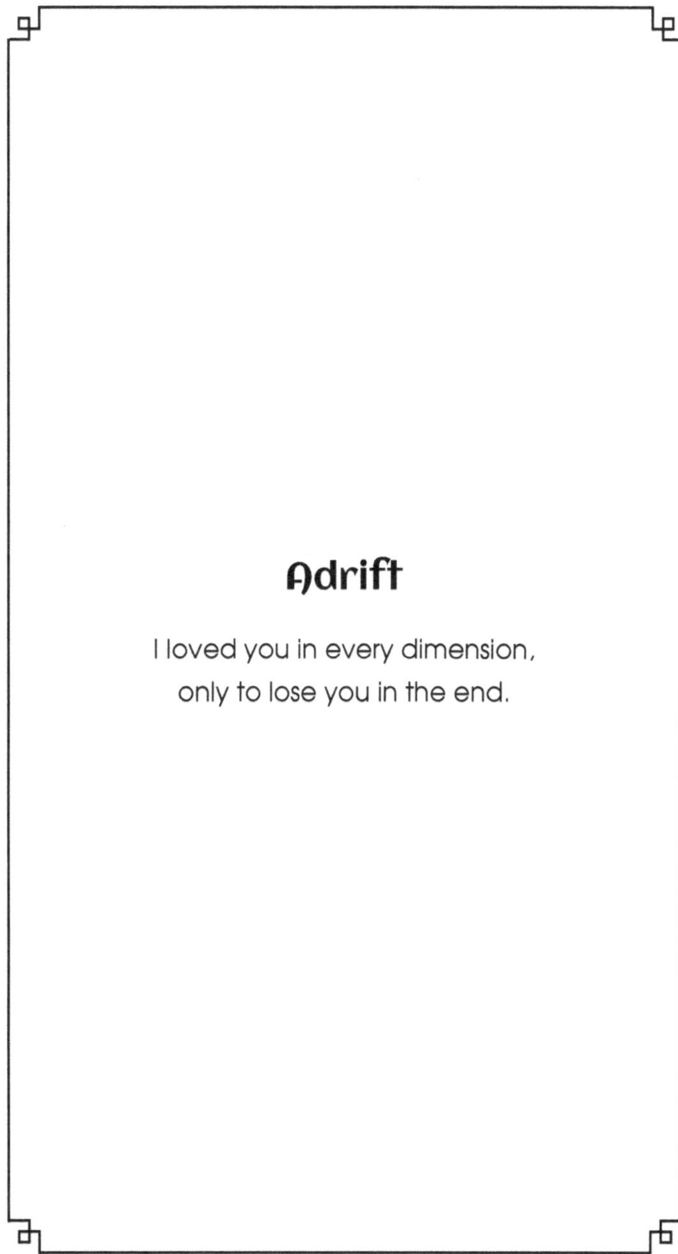

Adrift

I loved you in every dimension,
only to lose you in the end.

Forsaken Amour

Wind soughed the story of our love
amidst the trees,
the sky witnessed it,
the birds sang it
&
we buried it.

Élan Vital

The voice of demons within him,
kept drowning him in endless misery
and despair of darkness.
Yet,
a light shimmered within him,
which kept him going.

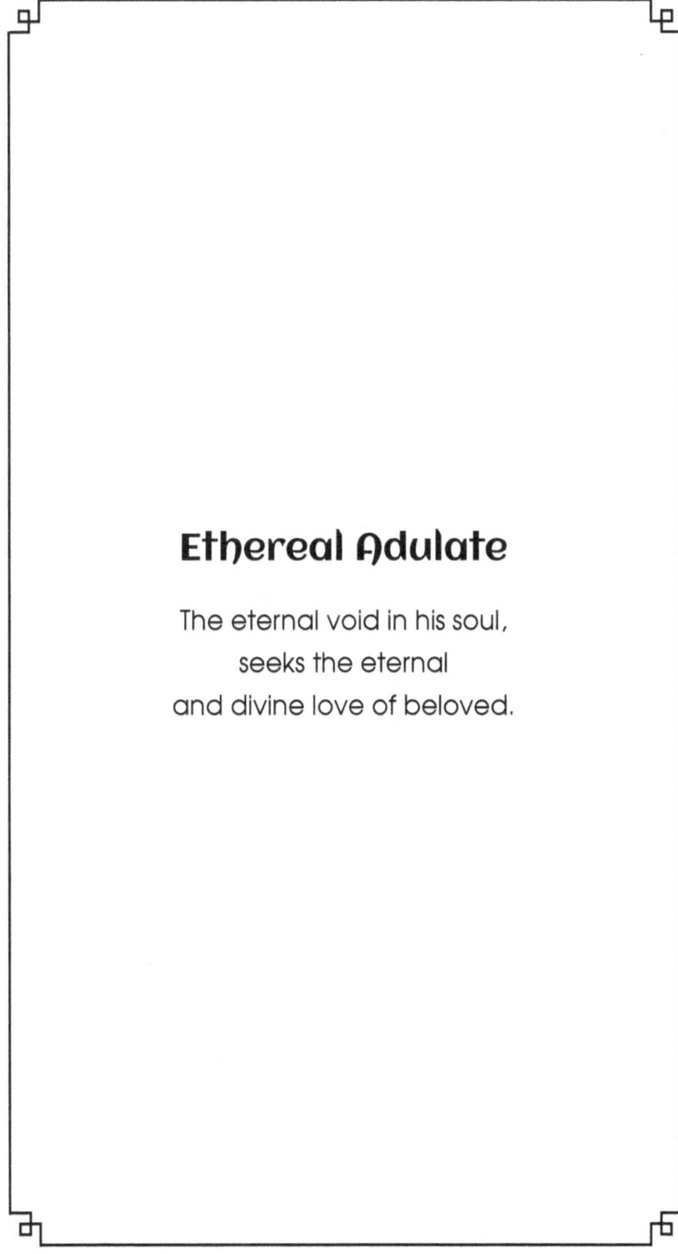

Ethereal Adulate

The eternal void in his soul,
seeks the eternal
and divine love of beloved.

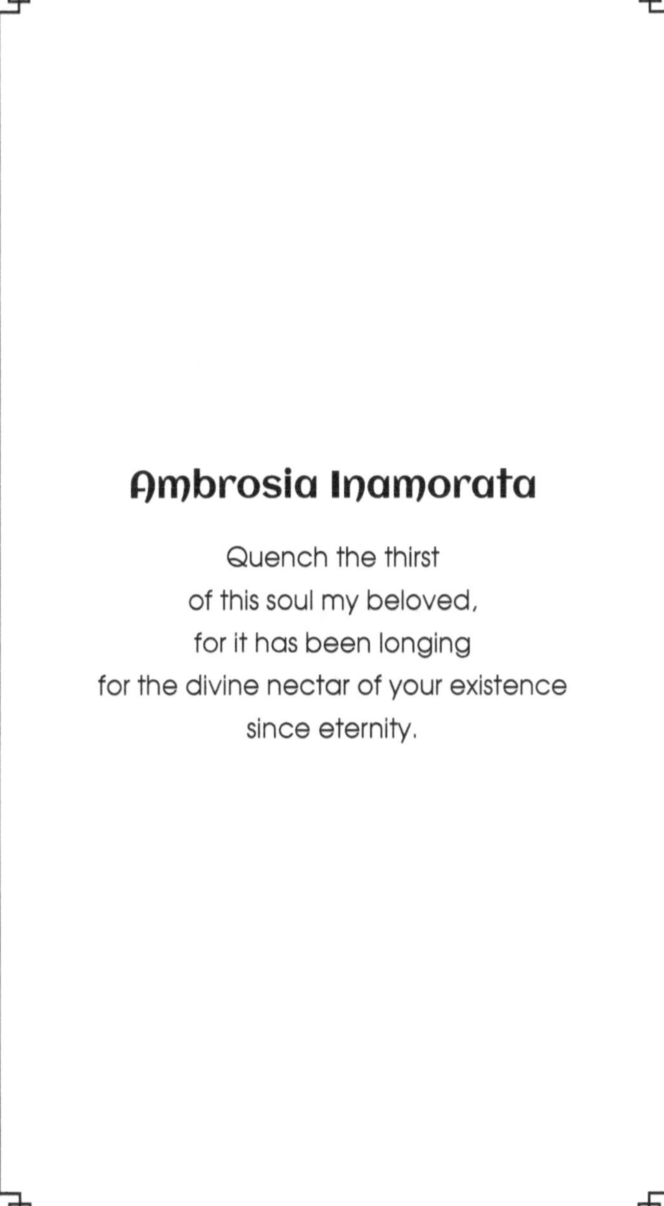

Ambrosia Inamorata

Quench the thirst
of this soul my beloved,
for it has been longing
for the divine nectar of your existence
since eternity.

Reverberation

A thousand words
are trapped deep within his being,
only to resonate it all back to him,
like an echo from a distant void.
Not to be heard by anyone,
as no one can fathom.

Within Me

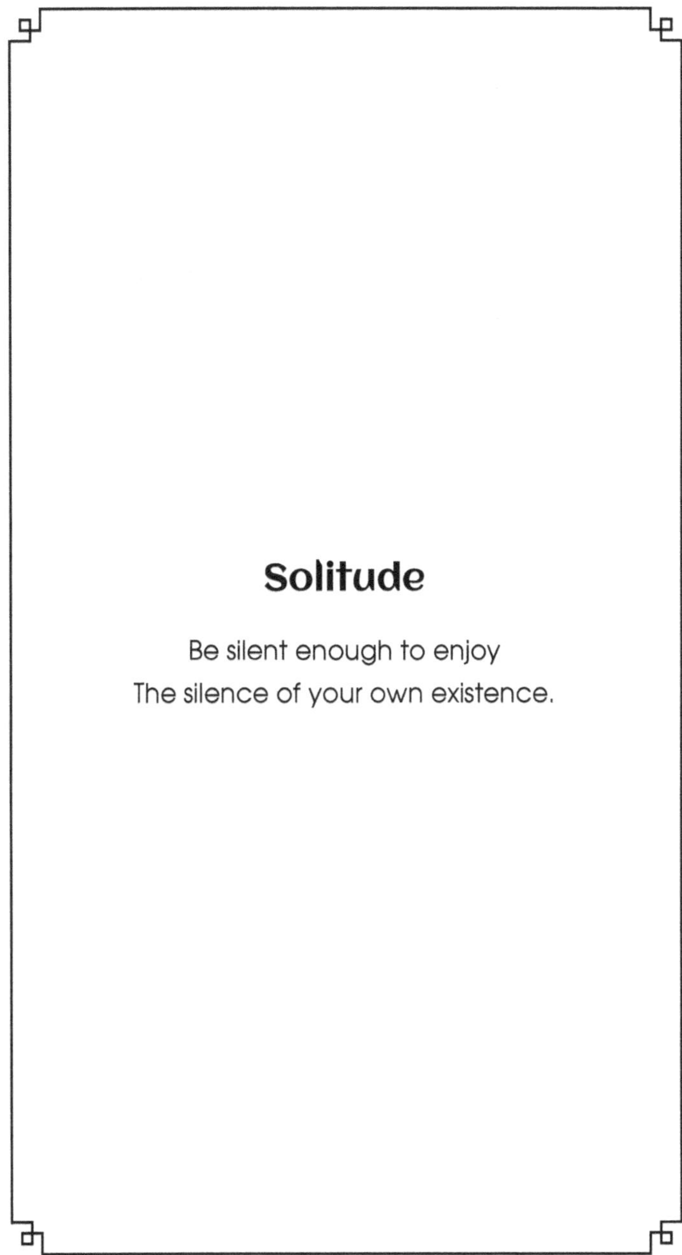

Solitude

Be silent enough to enjoy
The silence of your own existence.

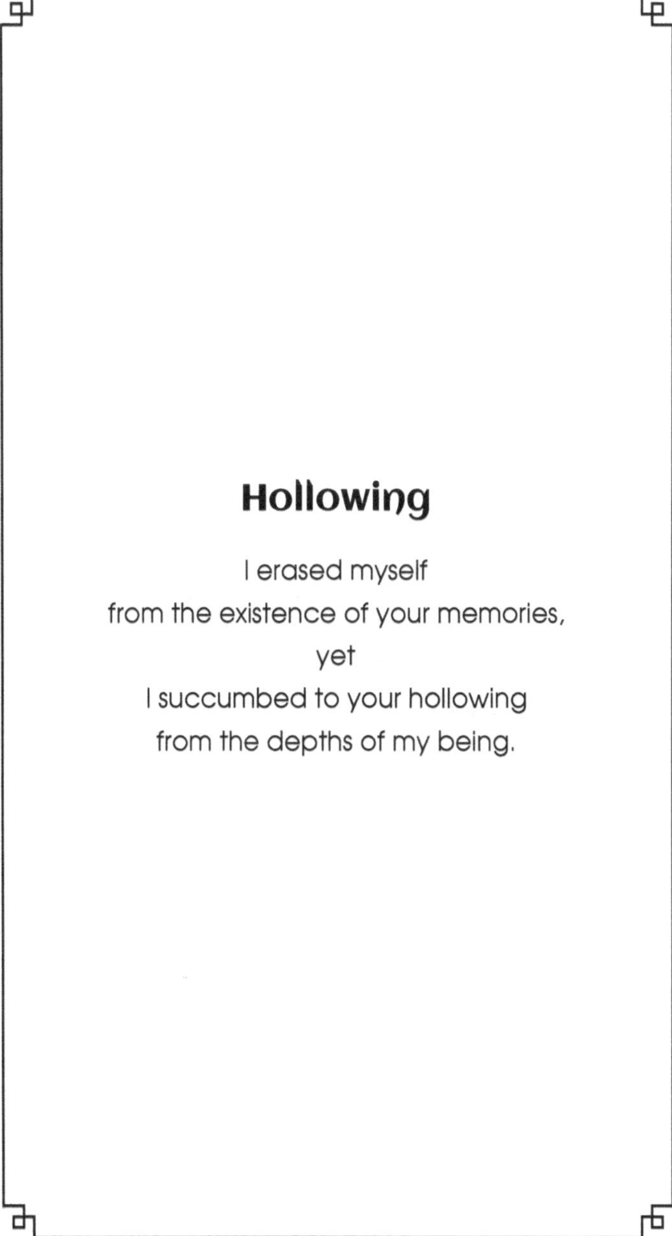

Hollowing

I erased myself
from the existence of your memories,
yet
I succumbed to your hollowing
from the depths of my being.

Mellifluous Divinity

In silence
I heard an euphonious voice
from depths of your being.
It was like a romance with cosmos
since time immemorial.

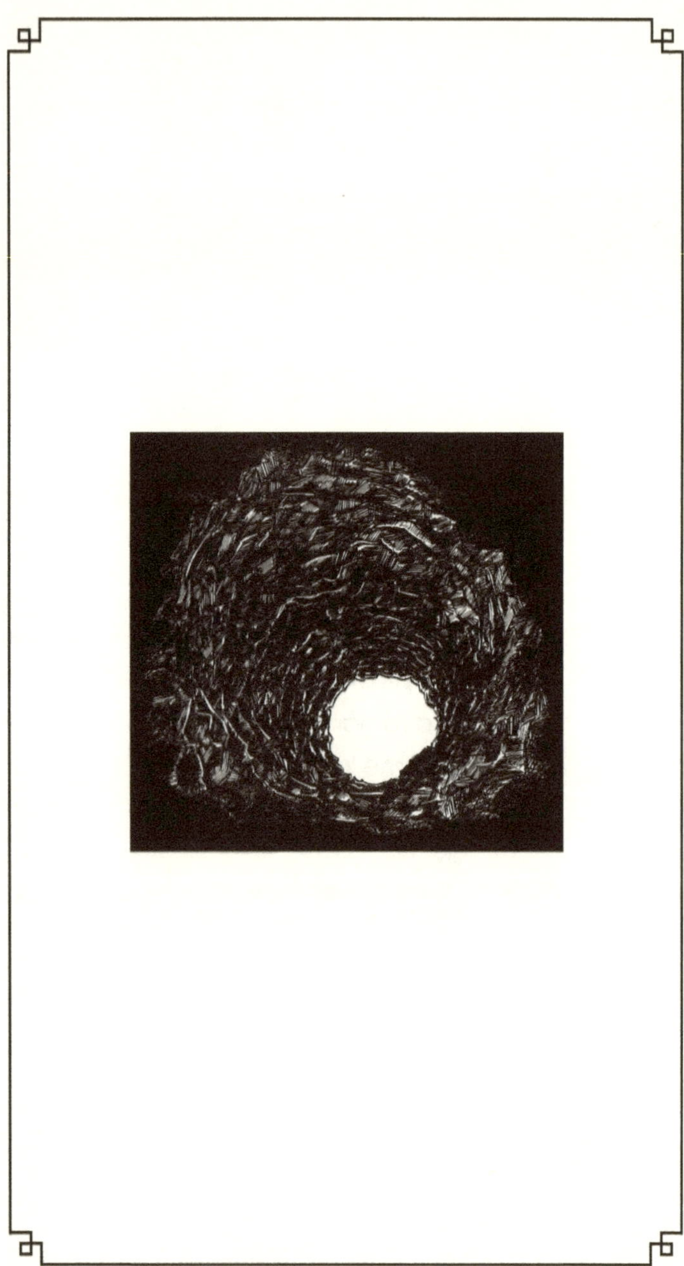

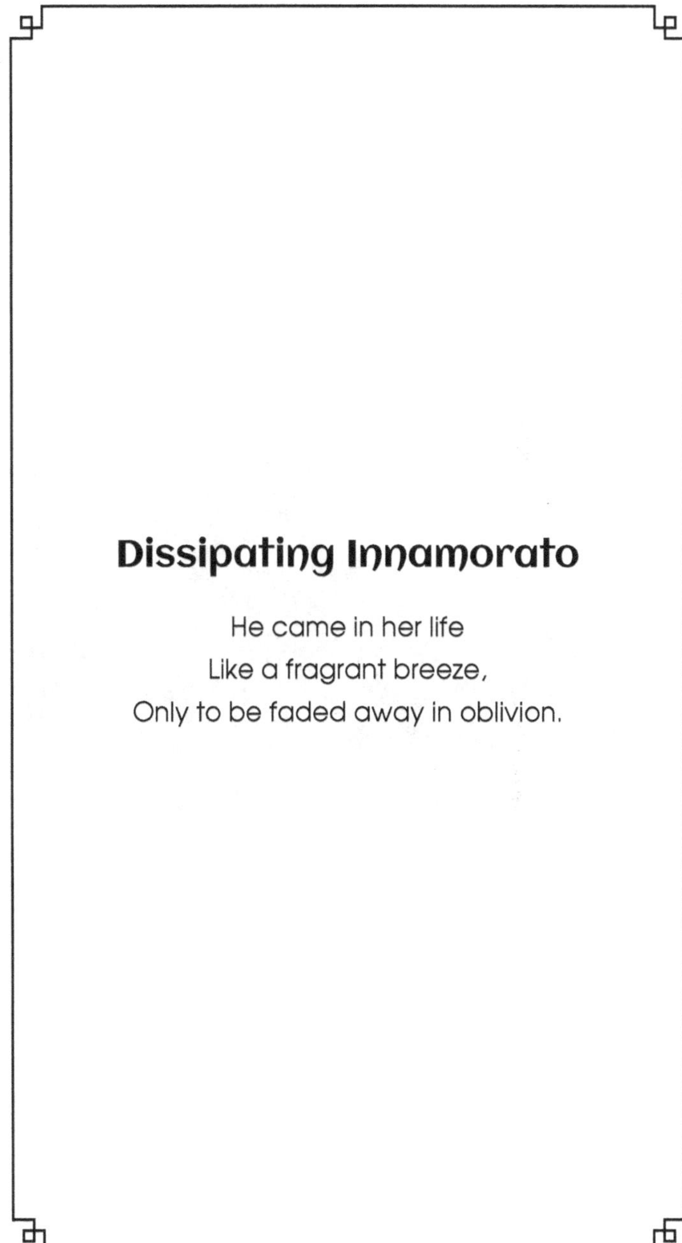

Dissipating Innamorato

He came in her life
Like a fragrant breeze,
Only to be faded away in oblivion.

Within Me

Within me, a universe unfolds.
Stories untold, mysteries unrevealed.
Loves tender touch, suffering stings.
Life's eternal dance within me, within me.